A Road to Self-Knowledge

AND

The Threshold of the Spiritual World

By RUDOLF STEINER

British Library Cataloguing-in-Publication Data
A catalogue record for this book is available from
the British Library

Contents

The Threshold of the Spiritual World

INTRODUCTORY REMARKS

IT is the endeavour of this treatise to convey knowledge concerning the being of man. The method of representation is arranged in such a way that the reader may grow into what is depicted, so that, in the course of reading, it becomes for him a kind of self-conference. If this soliloquy takes on such a form that thereby hitherto concealed forces, which can be awakened in every soul, reveal themselves, then the reading leads to a real inner work of the soul; and the latter can see itself gradually urged on to that soul-journeying, which truly advances towards the beholding of the spiritual world. What has to be imparted, therefore, has been given in the form of eight Meditations, which can be actually practised. If this is done, they can be adapted for bringing about in the soul, through its own inner deepening, that about which they speak.

It has been my aim on the one hand, to give something to those readers who have already made themselves conversant with the literature dealing with the domain of the supersensible, as it is here understood. Thus through the style of the description, through the communication directly connecting with the soul's experience, perhaps those who have knowledge of supersensible life will here find something that may appear of importance to them. On the other hand, many an one can find that just through this method of representation profit may be gained by those who yet stand far distant from the achievements of Spiritual Science.

Although this work is intended as an amplification of my other writings in the domain of Spiritual Science, it should nevertheless be possible to read it independently.

It has been my endeavor in my books, Theosophy and Occult Science, to represent the things as they show themselves to human observation, when it ascends to the Spiritual. In these works the method of representation is descriptive and its direction prescribed by conformity to the law manifesting out of the things themselves. In this, A Road to Self-Knowledge, the method of representation is different. Herein is stated that which can be experienced by a soul which sets out on the path to the Spirit in a certain manner. The treatise may therefore be regarded as an account of experiences of the soul; only it must be taken into consideration that the experiences which can be gained in such a way as is here described, must assume an individual form in each soul according to its own peculiarity. It has been my endeavour to do justice to this fact, so that one can also imagine that what is depicted here has been actually lived through by an individual soul, exactly as represented. The title of this treatise is, therefore A Road to Self-Knowledge. On that account it may serve the purpose of assisting other souls to live into this portrayal and attain to corresponding goals, and is an amplification of my book, Knowledge of the Higher Worlds and its Attainment.

Only isolated fundamental experiences of a spiritual scientific nature are represented. The giving of information in this manner of the further spheres of "Spiritual Science" is suspended for the present.

RUDOLF STEINER.

August 1912.

"Knowledge of the Higher Worlds and its Attainment" is a Revised and Enlarged Edition of "The Way of Initiation" with "Initiation and its Results."

A Road to Self-Knowledge

A Road to Self-Knowledge

FIRST MEDITATION

In which the Attempt is made to obtain a True Idea of the Physical Body

WHEN the soul is plunged into the phenomena of the outer world by means of physical perception, it cannot be said—after true self-analysis—that the soul perceives these phenomena, or that it actually experiences the things of the outer world. For, during the time of surrender, in its devotion to the outer world, the soul knows in truth nothing of itself. The fact is rather that the sunlight itself, radiating from things through space in various colours, lives or experiences itself within the soul. When the soul enjoys any event, at the moment of enjoyment it actually is joy in so far as it is conscious of being anything. Joy experiences itself in the soul. The soul is one with its experience of the world. It does not experience itself as something separate which feels joy, admiration, delight, satisfaction, or fear. It actually is joy, admiration, delight, satisfaction, and fear. If the soul would always admit this fact, then and only then would the occasions when it retires from the experience of the outer world and contemplates itself by itself appear in the right light. These moments would then appear as forming a life of quite a special character, which at once shows itself to be entirely different from the ordinary life of the soul. It is with this special kind of life that the riddles of psychic existence begin to dawn upon our consciousness. And these riddles are, in fact, the source of all other riddles of the world. For two worlds—an outer and an inner—present themselves to the spirit of man, directly the soul for a longer or shorter time ceases to be one with the outer world and withdraws into the loneliness of its own existence.

Now this withdrawal is no simple process, which, having been once accomplished, may be repeated again in much the same way. It is much more like the beginning of a pilgrimage into worlds previously unknown. When once this pilgrimage has been begun, every step made will call forth others, and will also be the preparation for these others. It is the first step which makes the soul capable of taking the next one. And each step brings fuller knowledge of the answer to the question: "What is Man in the true sense of the word?" Worlds open up which are hidden from the ordinary conception of life. And yet only in those worlds can the facts be found which will reveal the truth about this very conception. And even if no answer proves all-embracing and final, the answers obtained through the soul's inner pilgrimage go beyond everything which the outer senses and the intellect bound up with them can ever give. For this "something more" is necessary to man, and he will find that this is so, when he really and earnestly analyses his own nature.

At the outset of such a pilgrimage through the realms of our own soul, hard logic, and common sense are necessary. They form a safe starting-point for pushing on into the supersensible realms, which the soul, after all, is yearning to reach. Many a soul would prefer not to trouble about such a starting-point, but rather jump straight into the supersensible realms; though every healthy soul, even if it has at first avoided such common-sense considerations as disagreeable, will always submit to them later. For however much knowledge of the supersensible worlds one may have obtained from another starting-point, one can only gain a firm footing therein through some such methods of reasoning as follow here.

In the life of the soul moments may come in which it says to itself: "You must withdraw from everything that an outer world

2

can give you, if you do not wish to be forced into confessing that you are only a 'non-Sense-being' experiencing itself; but this would make life impossible, because it is clear that what you perceive around you exists independently of you; it existed without you and will continue to exist without you. Why then do colours perceive themselves in you, whilst your perception may be of no consequence to them? Why do the forces and materials of the outer world build up your body? Careful thought will show that this body only acquires life as the outward manifestation of you. It is a part of the outer world transformed into you, and, moreover, you realise that it is necessary to you. Because, to begin with, you could have no inner experiences without your senses, which the body alone can put at your disposal. You would remain empty without your body, such as you are at the beginning. It gives you through the senses inner fulness and substance." And then all those reflections may follow which are essential to any human existence if it does not wish to get into unbearable contradiction with itself at certain moments which come to every human being. This body—as it exists at the present moment—is the expression of the soul's experience. Its processes are such as to allow the soul to live through it and to gain experience of itself in it.

A time will come, however, when this will not be so. The life in the body will some day be subject to laws quite different from those which it obeys to-day whilst living for you, and for the sake of your soul's experience. It will become subject to those laws, according to which the material and forces in nature are acting, laws which have nothing more to do with you and your life. The body to which you owe the experience of your soul, will be absorbed in the general world-process and exist there in a form which has nothing more in common with anything that you experience within yourself.

Such a reflection may call forth in the inner experience all the horror of the thought of death, but without the admixture of the merely personal feelings which are ordinarily connected with this thought. When such personal feelings prevail it is not easy to establish the calm, deliberate state of mind necessary for obtaining knowledge. It is natural that man should want to know

3

about death and about a life of the soul independent of the dissolution of the body. But the relation existing between man himself and these questions is—perhaps more than anything else in the world—apt to confuse his objective judgment and to make him accept as genuine answers only those which are inspired by his own desires or wishes. For it is impossible to obtain true knowledge of anything in the spiritual realms without being able with complete unconcern to accept a "No" quite as willingly as a "Yes." And we need only look conscientiously into ourselves to become distinctly aware of the fact that we do not accept the knowledge of an extinction of the life of the soul together with the death of the body with the same equanimity as the opposite knowledge which teaches the continued existence of the soul beyond death. No doubt there are people who quite honestly believe in the annihilation of the soul on the extinction of the life of the body, and who arrange their lives accordingly. But even these are not unbiased with regard to such a belief. It is true that they do not allow the fear of annihilation, and the wish for continued existence, to get the better of the reasons which are distinctly in favour of such annihilation. So far the conception of these people is more logical than that of others who unconsciously construct or accept arguments in favour of a continued existence, because there is an ardent desire in the secret depths of their souls for such continued existence. And yet the view of those who deny immortality is no less biased, only in a different way. There are amongst them some who build up a certain idea of what life and existence are. This idea forces them to think of certain conditions, without which life is impossible. Their view of existence leads them to the conclusion that the conditions of the soul's life can no longer be present when the body falls away. Such people do not notice that they have themselves from the very first fixed an idea of the conditions necessary for the existence of life, and cannot believe in a continuation of life after death for the simple reason that, according to their own preconceived idea, there is no possibility of imagining an existence without a body. Even if they are not biased by their own wishes, they are biased by their own ideas from which they cannot emancipate themselves. Much confusion still prevails in such matters, and only a few examples need be put forward of the future possibilities that exist in this direction. For instance, the thought that the body, through whose processes the soul manifests its life, will eventually be given over to the outer world, and follow laws which have no relation to inner life—this idea puts the experience of death before the soul in such a way that no wish, no personal consideration, need necessarily enter the mind; and by a thought such as this we are led to a simple, impersonal question of abstract knowledge. Then also the thought will soon dawn upon the mind that the idea of death is not important in itself, but rather because it may throw light upon life. And we shall have to come to the conclusion that it is possible to understand the riddle of life through the nature of death.

The fact that the soul desires its own continued existence should, under all circumstances, make us suspicious with regard to any opinion which the soul forms about its own immortality. For why should the facts of the world pay any heed to the feelings of the soul? It is a possible thought that the soul, like a flame produced from fuel, merely flashes forth from the substance of the body and is then again extinguished. Indeed, the necessity of forming some opinion about its own nature might perhaps lead the soul to this very thought, with the result that it would feel itself to be devoid of meaning. But nevertheless this thought might be the actual truth of the matter, even although it made the soul feel itself to be meaningless.

When the soul turns its eyes to the body, it ought only to take into consideration that which the body may reveal to it. It then seems as if in nature such laws were active as drive matter and forces into a continual process of change, and as if these laws controlled the body and after a while drew it into that general process of mutual change between matter and forces.

You may put this idea in any way you like: it may be scientifically admissible, but with regard to true reality it proves itself to be quite impossible. You may find it to be the only idea which seems scientifically clear and sensible, and that all the rest are only subjective beliefs. You may imagine that it is so, but you cannot adhere to this idea with a really unbiased mind.

5

And that is the point. Not that which the soul according to its own nature feels to be a necessity, but only that which the outer world, to which the body belongs, makes evident, ought to be taken into consideration. After death this outer world absorbs the matter and forces of the body, which then follows laws that are quite indifferent to that which takes place in the body during life. These laws (which are of a physical and chemical nature) have just the same relation to the body as they have to any other lifeless thing of the outer world. It is impossible to imagine that this indifference of the outer world with regard to the human body should only begin at the moment of death, and should not have existed during life.

An idea of the relation between our body and the physical world cannot be obtained from life, but only from impressing upon our mind the thought that everything belonging to us as a vehicle of our senses, and as the means by which the soul carries on its life—all this is treated by the physical world in a way which only becomes clear to us, when we look beyond the limits of our bodily life and take into consideration that a time will come when we no longer have about us the body in which we are now gaining experience of ourselves. Any other conception of the relation between the outer physical world and the body conveys in itself the feeling of not conforming with reality. The idea, however, that it is only after death that the real relationship between the body and the outer world reveals itself does not contradict any real experience of the outer or the inner world.

The soul does not feel the thought to be unendurable, that the matter and the forces of its body are given up to processes of the outer world which have nothing to do with its own life. Surrendering itself to life in a perfectly unprejudiced way, it cannot discover in its own depths any wish arising from the body which makes the thought of dissolution after death a disagreeable one. The idea becomes unbearable only when it implies that the matter and the forces returning to the outer world take away with them the soul and its experiences of its own existence. Such an idea would be unbearable for the same reason as would any other idea, which does not grow naturally out of a reliance on the manifestation of the outer world.

6

To ascribe to the outer world an entirely different relation to the existence of the body during life from that which it bears after death is an absolutely futile idea. As such it will always be repelled by reality, whereas the idea that the relation between the outer world and the body remains the same before and after death is quite sound. The soul, holding this latter view, feels itself in perfect harmony with the evidence of facts. It is able to feel that this idea does not clash with facts which speak for themselves, and to which no artificial thought need be added.

One does not always observe in what beautiful harmony are the natural healthy feelings of the soul with the manifestations of nature. This may seem so self-evident as not to need any remark, and yet this seemingly insignificant fact is most illuminating. The idea that the body is dissolved into the elements has nothing unbearable in it, but on the other hand, the thought that the soul shares the fate of the body is senseless. There are many human personal reasons which prove this, but such reasons must be left out of consideration in objective investigation.

Apart from these reasons, however, thoroughly impersonal attention to the teachings of the outer world shows that no different influence upon the soul can be ascribed to this outer world before death from that which it has after death. The fact is conclusive that this idea presents itself as a necessity and holds its own against all objections which may be raised against it. Any one who thinks this thought when fully self-conscious feels its direct truth. In fact, both those who deny and those who believe in immortality think in this way. The former will probably say that the conditions of the bodily processes during life are involved in the laws which act upon the body after death; but they are mistaken if they believe that they are really capable of imagining these laws to be in a different relation to the body during life when it is the vehicle of the soul from that which prevails after death.

The only idea possible in itself is that the special combination of forces, which comes into existence with the body, remains quite as indifferent to the body in its character of a vehicle for the soul, as that combination of forces which produces the

7

processes in the dead body. This indifference is not existent on the part of the soul, but on the part of the latter and the forces of the body. The soul gains experience of itself by means of the body, but the body lives with, in, and through the outer world and does not allow any more importance to psychic phenomena than to those of the outer world. One comes to the conclusion that the heat and cold of the outer world have an influence upon the circulation of the blood in our body which is analogous to that of fear and shame which exist within the soul.

So, first of all, we feel within ourselves the laws of the outer world active in that special combination of materials which manifests itself as the form of the human body. We feel this body as a member of the outer world, but remain ignorant of its inner workings. External science of the present day gives some information as to how the laws of the outer world combine within that particular entity, which presents itself as the human body. We may hope that this information will grow more complete in the future. But such increasing information can make no difference whatever to the way in which the soul has to think of its relation to the body. It will, on the contrary, bring more and more into evidence that the laws of the outer world remain in the same relation to the soul before and after death. It is an illusion to expect that the progress of the knowledge of nature will show how far the bodily processes are agents of the life of the soul. We shall more and more clearly recognise that which takes place in the body during life, but the processes in question will always be felt by the soul as being outside it in the same way as the processes in the body after death.

The body must therefore appear within the outer world as a combination of forces and substances, which exists by itself and is explainable by itself as a member of this outer world. Nature causes a plant to grow and again decomposes it. Nature rules the human body, and causes it to pass away within her own sphere. If man takes up his position to nature with such ideas, he is able to forget himself and all that is in him and feel his body as a member of the outer world. If he thinks in such a way of its relations to himself and to nature, he experiences in connection with himself that which we may call his physical body.

SECOND MEDITATION

In which the Attempt is made to form a True Conception of the Elemental or Etheric Body

THROUGH the idea which the soul has to form in connection with the fact of death, it may be driven into complete uncertainty with regard to its own being. This will be the case when it believes that it cannot obtain knowledge from any other world but the world of the senses and from that which the intellect is able to ascertain about this world. The ordinary life of the soul directs its attention to the physical body. It sees that body being absorbed after death into the workshop of nature, which has no connection with that which the soul experiences before death as its own existence. The soul may know (through the preceding Meditation) that the physical body during life bears the same relation to nature as after death, but this does not lead it further than to the acknowledgment of the inner dependence of its own experiences up to the moment of death. What happens to the physical body after death is evident from observation of the outer world. But such observation is not possible with regard to its inner experience. In so far then as it perceives itself through the senses, the soul in its ordinary life cannot see beyond the boundary of death. If the soul is incapable of forming any ideas which go beyond that outer world which absorbs the body after death, then there is no possibility for it with regard to all which concerns its own being except to look into empty nothingness on the other side of death.

If this is to be otherwise, the soul must perceive the outer world by other means than those of the senses and of the intellect connected with them. These themselves belong to the body and decay together with it. What they tell us can lead to nothing but to the result of the first Meditation, and this result consists merely in the soul being able to say to itself: "I am bound to my body. This body is subject to natural laws which are related to me in the same way as all other natural laws. Through them I am a member of the outer world and a part of this world expressed in my body a fact which I realise most distinctly, when I consider what the outer world does to that body after death. During life it gives me senses and an intellect which make it impossible for me to see how matters stand with regard to my soul's experiences on the other side of death." Such a statement can only lead to two results. Either any further investigation into the riddle of the soul is suppressed and all efforts to obtain knowledge on this subject are given up; or else efforts are made to obtain by the inner experience of the soul that which the outer world refuses. These efforts may bring about an increase of power and energy with regard to this inner experience such as it would not have in ordinary life.

In ordinary life man has a certain amount of strength in his inner experiences, in his life of feeling and thought. He thinks, for instance, a certain thought as often as there is an inner or outer impulse to do so.

Any thought may, however, be chosen out of the rest and voluntarily repeated again and again without any outer reason, and with such intense energy as actually to make it live as an inner reality. Such a thought may by repeated effort be made the exclusive object of our inner experience. And while we do this we can keep away all outer impressions and memories which may arise in the soul. It is then possible to turn such a complete surrender to certain thoughts or feelings exclusive of all others, into a regular inner activity. If, however, such an inner experience is to lead to really important results, it must be undertaken according to certain tested laws. Such laws are recorded by the science of spiritual life. In my books The Way of Initiation and Initiation and its Results, a great number of these rules or laws are mentioned. Through such methods we obtain a strengthening of the powers of inner experience. This experience becomes in a certain way condensed. What is brought about by this we learn through that observation of ourselves which set in when the inner activity described has been continued for a sufficiently long time. It is true that much patience is required before convincing results appear. And if we are not disposed to exercise such patience for years, we shall obtain nothing of importance. Here it is only possible to give one example of such results, for they are of many varieties. And that which is mentioned here is adapted to further the particular method of meditation which we are now describing.

A man may carry out the inner strengthening of the life of his soul which has been indicated for a long period without perhaps anything happening in his inner life which is able to alter his usual way of thinking with regard to the world. Suddenly, however, the following may occur. Naturally the incident to be described might not occur in exactly the same way to two different persons. But if we arrive at a conception of one experience of this kind, we shall have gained an understanding of the whole matter in question. A moment may occur in which the soul gets an inner experience of itself in quite a new way. At the beginning it will generally happen that the soul during sleep wakes up, as it were, in a dream. But we feel at once that this experience cannot be compared with ordinary dreams. We are completely shut off from the world of sense and intellect, and yet we feel the experience in the same way as when we are standing fully awake before the outer world in ordinary life. We feel compelled to picture the experience ourselves. For this purpose we use ideas such as we have in ordinary life, but we know very well that we are experiencing things different from those to which such ideas are normally attached. These ideas are only used as a means of expression for an experience which we have not had before, and which we are also able to know that it is impossible for us to have in ordinary life.

We feel, for instance, as though thunderstorms were all around us. We hear thunder and see lightning. And yet we know we are in our own room. We feel permeated by a force previously quite unknown to us. Then we imagine we see rents in the walls around us, and we feel compelled to say to ourselves or to some one we think is near us: "I am now in great difficulties, the lightning is going through the house and taking hold of me; I feel it seizing and dissolving me." When such a series of representations has been gone through, the inner experience passes back to ordinary soul-conditions. We find ourselves again in ourselves with the memory of the experience just undergone. If this memory is as vivid and accurate as any other, it enables us to form an opinion of the experience. We then immediately know that we have gone through something which cannot be experienced by any physical sense nor by ordinary intelligence, for we feel that the description just given and communicated to others or to ourselves is only a means of expressing the experience. Although the expression is a means of understanding the fact of the experience, it has nothing in common with it. We know that we do not need any of our senses in having such an experience.

One who attributes it to a hidden activity of the senses or of the brain, does not know the true character of the experience. He adheres to the description which speaks of lightning, thunder, and rents in the walls, and, therefore, he believes that this experience of the soul is only an echo of ordinary life. He must consider the thing as a vision in the ordinary sense of the word. He cannot thins otherwise. He does not take into consideration, however, that when one describes such an experience one only uses the words lightning, thunder, rents in the walls as pictures of that which has been experienced, and that one must not mistake the pictures for the experience itself. It is true that the thing appears as if one really saw these pictures. But one did not stand in the same relation to the phenomenon of the lightning in this case as when seeing a flash with the physical eye. The vision of the lightning is only something which, as it were, conceals the experience itself; one looks through the lightning to something beyond which is quite different, to something which cannot be experienced in the outer world of sense.

In order that a correct judgment may be made possible, it is necessary that the soul which has such experiences should, when

they are over, be on a thoroughly sound footing with regard to
the ordinary outer world. It must be able clearly to contrast what
it has undergone as a special experience, with its ordinary
experience of the outer world. Those who in ordinary life are
already disposed to be carried away by all kinds of wild
imaginings regarding things, are most unfit to form such a
judgment. The more sound—or one might say sober—a sense of
reality we have got the more likely we are to form a true and,
therefore, valuable judgment of such things. One can only attain
to confidence in supersensible experiences when one feels with
regard to the ordinary world that one clearly perceives its
processes and objects as they really are.

When all necessary conditions are thus fulfilled, and when we
have reason to believe that we have not been misled by an
ordinary vision, then we know that we have had an experience
in which the body was not transmitting perceptions. We have
had direct perception through the strengthened soul without the
body. We have gained the certainty of an experience when
outside the body.

It is evident that in this sphere the natural differences between
fancy or illusioii and true observation made when outside the
body, cannot be indicated in any other way than in the realm of
outer sense-perception. It may happen that some one has a very
active imagination with regard to taste, and therefore, at the
mere thought of lemonade, gets the same sensation as if he were
really drinking it. The difference, however, in such a case
becomes evident through the association of actual circumstances
in life. And so it is also with those experiences which are made
when we are out of the body. In order to arrive at a fully
convincing conception in this sphere, it is necessary that we
should become familiar with it in a perfectly healthy way and
acquire the faculty of observing the details of the experience and
correcting one thing by another.

Through such an experience as the one described, we gain the
possibility of observing that which belongs to our proper self not
only by means of the senses and intellect—in other words, the
bodily instruments. Now we not only know something more of
the world than those instruments will allow of, but we know it in

13

a different way. This is especially important. A soul that passes through an inner transformation will more and more clearly comprehend that the oppressive problems of existence cannot be solved in the world of sense because the senses and the intellect cannot penetrate deeply enough into the world as a whole. Those souls penetrate deeper which so transform themselves as to be able to have experiences when outside the body; and it is in the records which they are able to give of their experiences that the means for solving the riddles of the soul can be found.

Now an experience that occurs when outside the body is of a quite different nature from one made when in the body. This is shown by the very opinion which may be formed about the experiences described, when, after it is over, the ordinary waking condition of the soul is re-established and memory has come into a vivid and clear condition. The physical body is felt by the soul as separated from the rest of the world, and seems only to have a real existence in so far as it belongs to the soul. It is not so, however, with that which we experience within ourselves and with regard to ourselves when outside the body, for then we feel ourselves linked to all that may be called the outer world. All our surroundings are felt as belonging to us just as our hands do in the world of sense. There is no indifference to the world outside us when we come to the inner soul-world. We feel ourselves completely grown together, and woven into one with that which here may be called the world. Its activities are actually felt streaming through our own being. There is no sharp boundary line between an inner and an outer world. The whole environment belongs to the observing soul just as our two physical hands belong to our physical head.

In spite of this, however, we may say that a certain part of this outer world belongs more to ourselves than the rest of the environment, in the same way in which we speak of the head as independent of the hands or feet. Just as the soul calls a piece of the outer physical world its body, so when living outside the body it may also consider a part of the supersensible outer world as belonging to it. When we penetrate to an observation of the realm accessible to us beyond the world of the senses, we may very well say that a body unperceived by the senses belongs to us. We may call this body the elemental or etheric body, but in using the word "etheric" we must not allow any connection with that fine matter which science calls "ether" to establish itself in our mind.

Just as the mere reflection upon the connection between man and the outer world of nature leads to a conception of the physical body which agrees with facts, so does the pilgrimage of the soul into realms that can be perceived outside the physical body lead to the recognition of an elemental or etheric body.

THIRD MEDITATION

In which the Attempt is made to form an Idea of Clairvoyant Cognition of the Elemental World.

WHEN we have perceptions by means of the elemental body and not through the physical senses, we experience a world that remains unknown to perception of the senses and to ordinary intellectual thinking. If we wish to compare this world with something belonging to ordinary life, we shall find nothing more appropriate than the world of memory. Just as recollections emerge from the innermost soul, so also do the supersensible experiences of the elemental body. In the case of a memory-picture the soul knows that it is related to an earlier experience in the world of the senses. In a similar way the supersensible conception implies a relation. Just as the recollection by its very nature presents itself as something which cannot be described as a mere picture of the imagination, so does also the supersensible conception. The latter bursts forth from the soul's experience, but manifests itself immediately as an inner experience that is related to something external. It is by means of recollection that a past experience becomes present to the soul. But it is by means of a supersensible conception that something, which at some time can be found somewhere in the supersensible world, becomes an inner experience of the soul. The very nature of supersensible conceptions impresses upon our mind that they are to be looked upon as communications from a supersensible world manifesting within the soul.

How far we get in this way with our experiences in the supersensible world depends upon the amount of energy we apply to the strengthening of the life of our soul.

The attainment of the conviction that a plant is not merely that which we perceive in the world of the senses as well as the attainment of such a conviction with regard to the whole earth belongs to the same sphere of supersensible experience. If any one, who has acquired the faculty of perception when outside his physical body, looks at a plant, he will be able to perceive—beside that which his senses are showing him—a delicate form which permeates the plant. This form presents itself as an entity of force; and he is brought to consider this entity as that which builds up the plant from the materials and forces of the physical world, and which brings about the circulation of the sap. He may say—employing an available, although not an altogether appropriate simile—that there is something in the plant which sets the sap in motion in the same way as that in which his own soul moves his arm. He looks upon something internal in the plant, and he must allow a certain independence to this inner principle of the plant in its relation to that part which is perceived by the senses. He must also admit that this inner principle existed before the physical plant existed. Then if he continues to observe how a plant grows, withers, and produces seeds, and how new plants grow out of these, he will find the supersensible form of energy especially powerful, when he observes these seeds. At this period the physical being is insignificant in a certain respect, whereas the supersensible entity is highly differentiated and contains everything that, from the supersensible world, contributes to the growth of the plant.

Now in the same way by supersensible observation of the whole earth we discover an entity of force which we can know with absolute certainty existed before everything came into being which is perceptible by the senses upon and within the earth. In this way we arrive at an experience of the presence of those supersensible forces which co-operated in forming and developing the earth in the past. What is thus experienced we may just as well call the etheric or elemental root-entities or bodies of the plant and of the earth, as we call the body through which we gain perception when outside the body, our own elemental or etheric body.

Even when we first begin to be able to observe in a supersensible way, we can assign elemental root-entities of this kind to certain things and processes apart from their ordinary qualities, which are perceptible in the world of the senses. We are able to speak of an etheric body belonging to the plant or to the earth. However, the elemental beings observed in this way are not by any means the only ones which reveal themselves to supersensible experience. We characterise the elemental body of a plant by saying that it builds up a form from the materials and forces of the physical world and thereby manifests its life in a physical body. But we may also observe beings that lead an elemental existence without manifesting their life in a physical body. Thus entities that are purely elemental are revealed to supersensible observation. It is not merely that we experience an addition, as it were, to the physical world; we experience another world in which the world of the senses presents itself as something which may be compared to pieces of ice floating about in water. A man who could only see the ice and not the water might quite possibly ascribe reality to the ice only and not to the water. Similarly, if we only take into account that which manifests itself to the senses, we may deny the existence of the supersensible world, of which the world of the senses is in reality a part, just as the floating pieces of ice are part of the water in which they are floating.

Now we shall find that those who are able to make supersensible observations describe what they behold by making use of expressions borrowed from the perceptions of sense. Thus we may find the elemental body of a being in the world of the senses, or that of a purely elemental being described as manifesting itself as a self-contained body of light and having manifold colours. These colours flash forth, glow or shine, and it appears that these phenomena of light and colour are the manifestation of its life. But that of which the observer is really speaking is altogether invisible, and he is perfectly aware that the light or colour-picture which he gives, has no more to do with that which he actually perceives than, for instance, the writing in which a fact is communicated has to do with the fact itself. And yet the supersensible experience has not been expressed through arbitrarily chosen perceptions of the senses. The picture seen is actually before the observer, and is similar to an impression of the senses. This is so because, during supersensible experiences liberation from the physical body is not complete. The physical body is still connected with the elemental body, and reduces the supersensible experience to a form perceptible to the senses. Thus the description given of an elemental being is given in the form of a visionary or fantastic combination of sense-impressions. But in spite of this, it is, when given in this manner, a true rendering of what has been experienced. For we have really seen what we are describing. The mistake that may be made is not in describing the vision as such, but in taking the vision for reality, instead of that to which the vision points: namely, the reality underlying it. A man who has never seen colours—a man born blind—will not, when he attains to the corresponding faculty of perception, describe elemental beings in such a way as to speak of flashing colours. He will make use of expressions familiar to him. To people, however, who are able to see physically, it is quite appropriate when they, in their description, make use of some such expression as the flashing forth of a colour form. By its aid they can give an impression of what has been seen by the observer of the elemental world. And this holds good not only for communications made by a clairvoyant—that is to say, one who is able to perceive by the aid of his elemental body—to a non-clairvoyant, but also for the intercommunication between clairvoyants themselves. In the world of the senses man lives in his physical body, and this body clothes the supersensible observations in forms perceptible to the senses. Therefore the expression of supersensible observations by making use of the sense-pictures they produce is, in ordinary earth-life, a useful means of communication.

The point is, that any one receiving communication experiences in his soul something bearing the right relation to the fact in question. Indeed, the pictures are only communicated in order to call forth an experience. Such as they really are, they cannot be found in the outer world. That is their main characteristic and also the reason why they call forth experiences that have no relation to anything material.

At the beginning of his clairvoyance, the pupil will find it difficult to become independent of the picture. When his faculty becomes more developed, however, a craving will arise for inventing more arbitrary means of communicating what has been seen. These will involve the necessity for explaining the signs which he uses. The more the exigencies of our time demand the general diffusion of supersensible knowledge, the greater will be the necessity for clothing such knowledge in the expressions used in everyday life on the physical plane.

Now supersensible experiences may come upon the pupil of themselves. And he has then the opportunity of learning something about the supersensible world by personal experience according as he is more or less often favoured, as we may say, by that world through its shining into the ordinary life of his soul. A higher faculty is that of calling forth at will clairvoyant perception from the latter. The path to the attainment of the faculty results ordinarily from energetic continuation of the inner strengthening of the soul-life, but much also depends upon establishing a certain keynote in the soul. A calm unruffled attitude of mind is necessary when confronting the supersensible world—an attitude which is as far removed on the one hand from the burning desire to experience the most possible in the clearest possible manner as it is from an entire lack of interest in that world. Burning desire has the effect of diffusing something like an invisible mist before the clairvoyant sight, whilst lack of interest acts in such a way that though the supersensible facts really do manifest themselves, they are simply not noticed. This lack of interest shows itself now and then in a very peculiar form. There are persons who honestly wish for supersensible experiences, but they form a priori a certain definite idea of what these experiences should be in order to be acknowledged as real. Then when the real experiences arrive, they flit by without being met by any interest, just because they are not such as they have imagined that they ought to be.

In the case of voluntarily produced clairvoyance there comes

20

a moment in the course of the soul's inner activity when we know; now my soul is experiencing something that it never experienced before. The experience is not a definite one, but a general feeling that we are not confronting the outer world of the senses, nor are we within it, nor yet are we within ourselves as in the ordinary life of the soul. The outer and inner experiences melt into one, into a feeling of life, hitherto unknown to the soul, concerning which, however, the soul knows that it could not be felt if it were only living within the outer world by means of the senses or by its ordinary feelings and recollections. We feel, moreover, that during this condition of the soul something is penetrating into it from a world hitherto unknown. We cannot, however, arrive at a conception of this unknown something. We have the experience but can form no idea of it. Now we shall find that when we have such an experience we get a feeling as if there were a hindrance in our physical bodies preventing us from forming a conception of that which is penetrating into the soul. If, however, we continue the inner efforts of our soul we shall, after a while, feel that we have overcome our own corporeal resistance. The physical apparatus of the intellect had hitherto only been able to form ideas in connection with experiences in the world of the senses. It is at the outset incapable of producing as an idea that which wants to manifest itself from out of the supersensible world. It must first be so prepared as to be able to do this. In the same way as a child is surrounded by the outer world, but has to have his intellectual apparatus prepared by experience in that world before he is able to form ideas of his surroundings, so is mankind in general unable to form an idea of the supersensible world. The clairvoyant who wishes to make progress prepares his own apparatus for forming ideas so that it will work on a higher level in exactly the same way as that of a child is prepared to work in the world of the senses. He makes his strengthened thoughts work upon this apparatus and as a consequence the latter is by degrees remodelled. It becomes capable of including the supersensible world in the realm of its ideas.

Thus we feel how through the activity of the soul we can

influence and remodel our own body. In the beginning the body acts as a strong counterpoise to the life of the soul; we feel it as a foreign body within us. But presently we notice how it always adapts itself more and more to the experiences of the soul; until, finally, we do not feel it any more at all, but find before us the supersensible world, just as we do not notice the existence of the eye with which we look upon the world of colours. The body then must become imperceptible before the soul can behold the supersensible world.

When we have in this way deliberately arrived at making the soul clairvoyant, we shall, as a rule, be able to reproduce this state at will if we concentrate upon some thought that we are able to experience within ourselves in a specially powerful manner. As a consequence of surrendering ourselves to such a thought we shall find that clairvoyance sets in. At first we shall not be able to see anything definite which we especially wish to see. Supersensible things or happenings for which we are in no way prepared, or desire to call forth, will play into the life of the soul. Yet, by continuing our inner efforts, we shall also attain to the faculty of directing the spiritual eye to such things as we wish to investigate. When we have forgotten an experience we try to bring it back to our memory by recalling to the mind something connected with the experience; and in the same way we may, as clairvoyants, start from an experience which we may rightly think is connected with what we want to find. In surrendering ourselves with intensity to the known experience, we shall often after a longer or shorter lapse of time find added thereto that experience which it was our object to attain. In general, however, it is to be noted that it is of the very greatest importance for the clairvoyant quietly to wait for the propitious moment. We should not desire to attract anything. If a desired experience does not arrive, it is best to give up the search for a while and to try to get an opportunity another time. The human apparatus of cognition needs to develop calmly up to the level of certain experiences. If we have not the patience to await such development, we shall make incorrect or inaccurate observations.

FOURTH MEDITATION

In which the Attempt is made to form a Conception of the Guardian of the Threshold

WHEN the soul has attained the faculty of making observations whilst remaining outside the physical body, certain difficulties may arise with regard to its emotional life. It may find itself compelled to take up quite a different position towards itself from that to which it was formerly accustomed. The soul was accustomed to regard the physical world as outside itself, while it considered all inner experience as its own particular possession. To supersensible surroundings, however, it cannot take up the same position as to the outer world. As soon as the soul perceives the supersensible world around it, it must merge itself therein to a certain extent: it cannot consider itself as separate from these surroundings as it does from the outer world. Through this fact all that can be designated as our own inner world in relation to the supersensible surroundings assumes a certain character which is not easily reconcilable with the idea of inward privacy. We can no longer say, "I think," "I feel," or "I have my thoughts and fashion them as I like." But we must say instead, "Something thinks in me, something makes emotions flash forth in me, something forms thoughts and compels them to come forward in an absolutely definite way and make their presence felt in my consciousness."

Now this feeling may contain something exceedingly depressing when the manner in which the supersensible

23

experience presents itself is such as to convey the certainty that we are actually experiencing a reality and are not losing ourselves in imaginary fancies or illusions. Such as it is it may indicate that the supersensible surrounding world wants to feel, and to think for itself, but that it is hindered in the realisation of its intention. At the same time we get a feeling that that which here wants to enter the soul is the true reality and the only one that can give an explanation of all we have hitherto experienced as real. This feeling also gives the impression that the supersensible reality shows itself as something which in value infinitely transcends the reality hitherto known to the soul. This feeling is therefore depressing, because it makes us feel that we are actually forced to will the next step which has to be taken. It lies in the very nature of that which we have become through our own inner experience to take this step. If we do not take it we must feel this to be a denial of our own being, or even self-annihilation. And yet we may also have the feeling that we cannot take it, or if we attempt it as far as we can, it must remain imperfect.

All this develops into the idea: Such as the soul now is, a task lies before it, which it cannot master, because such as it now is, it is rejected by its supersensible surroundings, for the supersensible world does not wish to have it within its realm. And so the soul arrives at a feeling of being in contradiction to the supersensible world; and has to say to itself: "I am not such as to make it possible for me to mingle with that world, and yet only there can I learn the true reality and my relation to it; for I have separated myself from the recognition of Truth." This feeling means an experience which will make more and more clear and decisive the exact value of our own soul. We feel ourselves and our whole life to be steeped in an error. And yet this error is distinct from other errors. The others are thought; but this is a living experience. An error that is only thought may be removed when the wrong thought is replaced by the right one. But the error that has been experienced has become part of the life of our soul itself; we ourselves are the error, we cannot simply correct it, for, think as we will, it is there, it is part of reality, and that, too, our own reality. Such an experience is a crushing one for the "self." We feel our inmost being painfully rejected by all that we desire. This pain, which is felt at a certain stage in the pilgrimage of the soul, is far beyond anything which can be felt as pain in the physical world. And therefore it may surpass everything which we have hitherto become able to master in the life of our soul. It may have the effect of stunning us. The soul stands before the fearful question: Whence shall I gather strength to carry the burden laid upon me? And the soul must find that strength within its own life. It consists in something that may be characterised as inner courage, inner fearlessness.

In order now to be able to proceed further in the pilgrimage of the soul, we must have developed so far that the strength which enables us to trace our experiences will well up from within us and produce this inner courage and inner fearlessness in a degree never required for life in the physical body. Such strength is only produced by true self-knowledge. In fact it is only at this stage of development that we realise how little we have hitherto really known of ourselves. We have surrendered ourselves to our inner experiences without observing them as one observes a part of the outer world. Through the steps that have led to the faculty of extra-physical experience, however, we obtain a special means of self-knowledge. We learn in a certain sense to contemplate ourselves from a standpoint which can only be found when we are outside the physical body. And the depressing feeling mentioned before is itself the very beginning of true self-knowledge. To realise oneself as being in error in one's relations to the outer world is a sign that one is realising the true nature of one's own soul.

It is in the nature of the human soul to feel such enlightenment regarding itself as painful. It is only when we feel this pain that we learn how strong is the natural desire to feel ourselves, just as we are—to be human beings of importance and value. It may seem an ugly fact that this is so; but we have to face this ugliness of our own self without prejudice. We did not notice it before, just because we never consciously penetrated deeply enough into our own being. Only when we do so do we perceive how dearly we love that in ourselves which must be felt as ugly. The power of self-love shows itself in all its enormity. And at the same time we see how little inclination we have to lay aside this self-love. Even when it is only a question of those qualities of the soul which are concerned with our ordinary life and relations to other people, the difficulties turn out to be quite great enough. We learn, for instance, by means of true self-knowledge, that though we have hitherto believed that we felt kindly towards some one, nevertheless we are cherishing in the depths of our soul secret envy or hatred or some such feeling towards that person. We realise that these feelings, which have not as yet risen to the surface, will some day certainly crave for expression. And we see how very superficial it would be to say to ourselves: "Now that you have learned how it stands with you, root out your envy or hatred." For we discover that armed merely with such a thought we shall certainly feel exceedingly weak, when some day the craving to show our envy or to satisfy our hatred breaks forth with elemental power. Such special kinds of self-knowledge manifest themselves in different people according to the special constitution of their souls. They appear when experience outside the body begins, for then our self-knowledge becomes a true one, and is no longer troubled by any desire to find ourselves modelled in some such way as we should like to be.

Such special self-knowledge is painful and depressing to the soul, but if we want to attain to the faculty of experience outside the body, it cannot be avoided, for it is necessarily called forth by the special position which we must take up with regard to our own soul. For the very strongest powers of the soul are required, even if it is only a question of an ordinary human being obtaining self-knowledge in a general way. We are observing ourselves from a standpoint outside our previous inner life. We have to say to ourselves: "I have contemplated and judged the things and occurrences of the world according to my human nature. I must now try to imagine that I cannot contemplate and judge them in that way. But then I should not be what I am. I should be a mere nothing." And not only a man in the midst of ordinary everyday life, who only very rarely even thinks about the world or life, would have to address himself in this way.

26

Any man of science, or any philosopher, would have to do so. For even philosophy is only observation and judgment of the world according to individual qualities and conditions of human life. Now such a judgment cannot mingle with supersensible surroundings. It is rejected by them. And therewith everything we have been up to that moment is rejected. We must look back upon our whole soul, upon our ego itself, as upon something which has to be laid aside, when we want to enter the supersensible world. The soul, however, cannot but consider this ego as its real being until it enters the supersensible worlds. The soul must consider it as the true human being, and must say to itself: "Through this my ego I have to form ideas of the world. I must not lose this ego of mine if I do not want to give myself up as a being altogether." There is in the soul the strongest inclination to guard the ego at all points in order not to lose one's foothold absolutely. What the soul thus feels of necessity to be right in ordinary life, it must no longer feel when it enters supersensible surroundings. It has there to cross a threshold, where it must leave behind not only this or that precious possession, but that very being which it has hitherto believed itself to be. The soul must be able to say to itself: "That which until now has seemed to me to be my surest truth, I must now, on the other side of the threshold of the supersensible world, be able to consider as my deepest error."

Before such a demand the soul may well recoil. The feeling may be so strong that the necessary steps would seem a surrender of its own being, and an acknowledgment of its own nothingness, so that it admits more or less completely on the threshold its own powerlessness to fulfil the demands put before it. This acknowledgment may take all possible forms. It may appear merely as an instinct and seem to the pupil who thinks and acts upon it as something quite different from what it really is. He may, for instance, feel a great dislike to all supersensible truths. He may consider them as day dreams, or imaginary fancies. He does so only because in those depths of his soul of which he is ignorant he has a secret fear of these truths. He feels that he can only live with that which is admitted by his senses and his intellectual judgment. He therefore avoids arriving at the threshold of the supersensible world, and he veils the fact of his avoidance of it by saying: "That which is supposed to lie behind that threshold is not tenable by reason or by science." The fact is simply that he loves reason and science such as he knows them, because they are bound up with his ego. This is a very frequent form of self-love and cannot as such be brought into the supersensible world.

It may also happen that there is not only this instinctive halt before the threshold. The pupil may consciously proceed to the threshold and then turn back, because he fears that which lies before him. He will then not easily be able to blot out from the ordinary life of his soul the effect of thus approaching it. The effect will be that weakness will spread over the whole of his soul's life.

What ought to take place is this, that the pupil on entering the supersensible world should make himself able to renounce that which in ordinary life he considers as the deepest truth and to adapt himself to a different way of feeling and judging things. But at the same time he must keep in mind that when he again confronts the physical world, he must make use of the ways of feeling and judging that are suitable for this physical world. He must not only learn to live in two different worlds, but also to live in each in quite a different way, and he must not allow his sound judgment, which he needs for ordinary life in the world of reason and of the senses, to be encroached upon by the fact that he is obliged to make use of another kind of discernment while in another world.

To take up such a position is difficult for human nature, and the capacity for doing so is only acquired through continued energetic and patient strengthening of our psychic life. Any one who goes through the experiences of the threshold realises that it is a boon to the ordinary life of the soul not to be led so far. The feelings that awaken are such that one cannot but think that this boon proceeds from some powerful entity, who protects man from the danger of undergoing the dread of self-annihilation at the threshold. Behind the outer world of ordinary life there is another. Before the threshold of this world a stern guardian is standing, who prevents man from knowing what the laws of the supersensible world are. For all doubts and all uncertainty concerning that world are, after all, easier to bear than the sight of that which one must leave behind when we want to cross the threshold.

The pupil remains protected against the experience described, as long as he does not step forward to the very threshold. The fact that he receives descriptions of such experiences from those who have trodden or crossed this threshold does not change the fact of his being protected. On the contrary, such communications may be of good service to him when he approaches the threshold. In this case as in many others, a thing is done better if one has an idea of it beforehand. But as regards the self-knowledge which must be gained by a traveller in the supersensible world nothing is changed by such preliminary knowledge. It is therefore not in harmony with the facts, when many clairvoyants, or those acquainted with the nature of clairvoyance, assert that these things should not be mentioned at all to people who are not on the point of resolving to enter into the supersensible world. We are now living in a time when people must become more and more acquainted with the nature of the supersensible world, if the life of their soul is to become equal to the demands of ordinary life upon it. The spread of supersensible knowledge, including the knowledge of the guardian of the threshold, is one of the tasks of the moment and of the immediate future.

FIFTH MEDITATION

In which the Attempt is made to form an Idea of the Astral Body

WHEN we experience through our elemental body a surrounding supersensible world, we feel ourselves less separated from that world than we are from physical surroundings when in our physical body. And yet we bear a relation to these supersensible surroundings, which may be expressed by saying that we have attached to ourselves certain substances of the elemental world in the form of an elemental body, just as in the physical outer world we carry some of its materials and forces attached to us in the shape of our physical body. We observe that this is so when we want to find our way about in the supersensible world outside the physical body. It may happen that we have before us some fact or being of the supersensible world. It may be there, and we can behold it, but we do not know what it is. If we are strong enough, we may drive it away, but only by carrying ourselves back into the world of the senses by energetic concentration upon our experiences in that world. We are, however, unable to remain in the supersensible world and compare with other beings or facts the being or the fact perceived. And yet it is only by so doing that we could form a correct estimate of what is beheld. Thus our "sight" in the supersensible world may be limited to the perception of single things without the faculty of moving freely from one thing to another. We then feel fettered to that single

30

thing.

We may now look for the reason of this limitation. This can only be found when through further inner development the life of our soul has been still more strengthened and we arrive at a point when this limitation is no longer there. And then we shall discover that the reason why we could not move from one thing to another is to be found in our own soul. We learn that sight in the supersensible world differs in this way from perception in the world of the senses. One can, for instance, in the physical world see every visible thing when one has got sound eyes. If one sees one thing one can also, with the same eyes, see all other things. This is not so in the supersensible world. One can have the organ of supersensible perception developed in such a way that one can experience this or that fact, but if another fact is to be perceived one's organ must first be specially developed for this purpose. Such a development gives one the feeling that an organ has awoke to a particular region of the supersensible world. One feels as if one's elemental body were in a kind of sleep with regard to the supersensible world, and as if it had to be awoke with regard to each particular thing. It is in fact possible to speak of being asleep and being awake in the elemental world; but they are not alternate states as in the physical world. They are states existing in man simultaneously. As long as we have not attained any faculty for experience through our elemental body, that body is asleep. We always carry this body about with us, but it is a sleeping body. With the strengthening of the life of our soul the awakening begins, but at first only for a part of the elemental body. The more we awaken our elemental being, the deeper we penetrate into the elemental world.

In the elemental world itself there is nothing that can aid the soul to bring about this awakening. However much may be beheld, one thing perceived adds nothing to the possibility of perceiving another thing. Free movement in the supersensible world can be attained by the soul through nothing that is found in the elemental environment. When we continue the exercises to strengthen the soul, we attain more and more this power of moving in particular regions. Through all this our attention is

31

drawn to something in ourselves, which does not belong to the elemental world, but is discovered within ourselves through our experience of that world. We feel ourselves as particular beings in the supersensible world, who seem to be the rulers, directors, and masters of their elemental bodies, and who by and by awaken these bodies to supersensible consciousness.

When we have arrived so far, a feeling of intense loneliness overwhelms the soul. We find ourselves in a world that is elemental in all directions; we see only ourselves within endless elemental space as beings which can nowhere find their equal. It is not affirmed that every development to clairvoyance should lead to this fearful loneliness, but any one who consciously and by his own efforts acquires a strengthening of his soul, will meet with it. And if he follow a teacher who gives him directions from step to step in order to further his development, he will, perhaps late, but still some day, have to realise that his teacher has left him all to himself. He will find that his teacher has left him, and that he is abandoned to loneliness in the elemental world. Only afterwards will he understand that he has been obliged to let him depend upon himself since the necessity for such self-reliance had asserted itself.

At this stage of the soul's pilgrimage the pupil feels himself an exile in the elemental world. But now he can go on further if sufficient force has been aroused in him through his inner exercises. He may begin to see a new world emerge—not in the elemental world, but within himself—a world that is not one either with the pkysical or with the elemental world. For such a pupil a second supersensible world is added to the first. This second supersensible world is at first completely an inner world. The pupil feels that he carries it within himself and that he is alone with it. To compare this state to anything in the world of the senses, let us take the following case. Somebody has lost all his dear ones through death and now carries only the recollection of them in his soul. They live on for him only as his thoughts. He stands to this second supersensible world in such a way that he carried it within himself; but he knows that he is shut out from its reality. Nevertheless he feels that this reality within his soul, whatever it may be, is something much more

32

real than mere recollection from the world of the senses. This supersensible world lives an independent life within one's own soul. All that is there is yearning to get out of the soul, and arrive at something else. Thus one feels a world within oneself, but a world that does not want to remain there. This produces a feeling like being torn asunder by every separate detail of that world. One may arrive at a point where these details free themselves, where they break through something which seems like a psychic shell and escape. Then one may feel oneself the poorer by all that has in this manner torn itself away from the soul.

One now learns that that part of the supersensible reality in the soul which one is able to love for its own sake, and not simply because it is actually in one's own soul, behaves in a particular way. What one can thus love deeply does not tear itself from the soul; it certainly does force its way out of the soul, but carries the soul along with it. It carries the soul to that region where it lives in its true reality. A kind of union with the real essence takes place, for hitherto one has only carried something like a reflection of this real essence within one. The love here mentioned must, however, be of the kind that is experienced in the supersensible world. In the world of the senses one can only prepare oneself for such love. And this preparation takes place when one strengthens one's capacity for love in the world of the senses. The greater the love of which one is capable in the physical world, the more of this capacity remains for the supersensible world. With regard to the individual entities of the supersensible world, this works as follows. You cannot, for instance, get into touch with those real supersensible beings which are connected with the plants of the physical world if you do not love plants in the world of the senses, and so on. An error, however, may very easily arise with regard to such things. It may happen that somebody in the physical world passes the vegetable kingdom by with complete indifference, and yet an unconscious affinity for that kingdom may lie hidden in the soul. Afterwards when he enters the supersensible world this love may awaken.

But the union with beings in the supersensible world does not

33

only depend upon love. Other feelings, as, for instance, respect and reverence, which the soul may have for a being when it first feels the picture of this being arise within it, have the same effect. These qualities will, however, always be such as must be reckoned as belonging to the inner qualities of the soul. One will in this way learn to know those beings of the supersensible world to which the soul itself opened the way through such inner qualities. A sure way to get acquainted with the supersensible world consists in gaining access to the different beings through one's relationship to their reflections. In the world of the senses we love a being after having learned to know him; in the second supersensible world we may love the image of a being before meeting with the being itself, as this image presents itself before the meeting takes place.

That which the soul in this way learns to know within itself is not the elemental body. It stands in relation to that body as its "awakener." It is a being dwelling within the soul which is experienced in the same way as that in which you would experience yourself during sleep if you were not unconscious but felt yourself to be conscious when outside your physical body and in the position of its "awakener" at the moment of its rousing from sleep. Thus the soul learns to know a being within itself which is a third something beside the physical and the elemental bodies. Let us call this something the astral body, and this expression shall, for the time being, mean nothing but that which in the way described is experienced within the second supersensible world.

SIXTH MEDITATION

In which the Attempt is made to form a Conception of the Ego-Body or Thought-Body

THE feeling of being outside our physical body is stronger during experiences within the astral body than during those within the elemental body. In the case of the elemental body we feel ourselves outside the region in which the physical body exists, and yet we feel connected with the latter body. In the astral body we feel the physical body itself as something outside our own being. On passing into the elemental body we feel something like an expansion of our own being; but in identifying our consciousness with the astral body it is as though we made a jump into another being. And we feel a world of spiritual beings sending their activities into that being. We feel ourselves in some way or other connected with or related to these beings. And by degrees we learn to know how these beings are mutually connected. To our human consciousness the world widens out in the direction of the spiritual. We behold spiritual beings, for example, who bring about the succession of epochs in the development of mankind so that we realise that the different characters of the different epochs are, as it were, stamped upon them by real spiritual entities. These are the Spirits of Time or Primordial Powers (Archai). We learn to know other beings, whose psychic life is such that their thoughts are at the same time active forces of nature. We are led to understand that only to physical perception do the forces of

35

nature appear to be constituted as physical perception imagines them to be. That in fact everywhere, where a force of nature is acting, the thought of some being is expressing itself just as a human soul finds expression in the movement of a hand. All this is not as though man by the aid of any theory is able in thought to place living beings at the back of nature's processes; when we realise ourselves in our astral body we enter into quite as concrete and real a relation to those beings as that between human individuals in the physical world. Among the spirits into whose realm we thus penetrate we discover a series of gradations, and we may thus speak of a world of higher hierarchies. Those beings whose thoughts manifest themselves to physical perception as forces of nature we may call Spirits of Form.

Experience in that world assumes that we feel our physical being as something outside us, in the same way as in physical existence we look upon a plant as a thing outside ourselves. We shall feel this state of being outside all that in ordinary life must be felt as the whole compass of our own being, as a very painful one, so long as it is not accompanied by a certain other experience. If the inner work of the soul has been energetically carried on and has led to a proper deepening and strengthening of the life of our soul, it is not necessary that this pain should be very pronounced. For a slow and gradual entrance into that second experience may be accomplished simultaneously with our entrance into the astral body as our natural vehicle.

This second experience will consist in obtaining the capacity for considering all that, which before filled and was connected with our own soul, as a kind of recollection, so that we stand in the same relation to our own former ego as we do to our recollections in the physical world. Only through such an experience do we attain to full consciousness of ourselves as truly living with our own real being in a world quite different from that of the senses. We now possess the knowledge that that which we carry about with us and have hitherto considered as our ego is something different from what we really are. We are now able to stand opposite to ourselves, and we may form an idea concerning that which now confronts our own soul and of

36

which it formerly said, "That is myself." Now the soul no longer says, "That is myself," but, "I am carrying that something about with me." Just as the ego in ordinary life feels independent of its own recollections, so our newly-found ego feels itself independent of our former ego. It feels that it belongs to a world of purely spiritual beings. And as this experience—a real experience: no mere theory—comes to us, so we realise what that really is which we hitherto considered as our ego. It presents itself as a web of recollections, produced by the physical, the elemental, and the astral bodies in the same way as an image is produced by a mirror. Just as little as a man identifies himself with his reflected picture, so little does the soul, experiencing itself in the spiritual world, identify itself with that which it experiences of itself in the world of the senses. The comparison with the reflected image is, of course, to be taken merely as a comparison. For the reflected image vanishes when we change our position with regard to the mirror. The web, woven of recollections and representing what we in the physical world consider as our own being, has a greater degree of independence than the image in the mirror. It has in a certain way a being of its own. And yet to the real being of the soul it is only like a picture of our real self. The real being of the soul feels that this picture is needed for the manifestation of its real self. This real being knows that it is something different, but also that it would never have attained to any real knowledge of itself if it had not at first realised itself as its own image within that world, which, after its ascent into the spiritual world, becomes an outer world.

The web of recollection which we now regard as our former ego may be called the "ego-body" or "thought-body." The word "body" must in this connection be taken in a wider sense than that which is usually called a "body." By "body" is here meant all that we experience as belonging to us and of which we do not say, "We are it," but, "We possess it."

Only when clairvoyant consciousness has arrived at the point where it experiences, as a sum of recollections, that which it formerly considered to be itself, does it become possible to acquire real experience of what is hidden behind the phenomenon of death. For then we have arrived at a truly real world in which we feel ourselves as beings who are able to retain, as though in a memory, what has been experienced in the world of the senses. This sum total of experiences in the physical world needs—in order to continue its existence—a being who is able to retain it in the same way in which the ordinary ego retains its recollections. Supersensible knowledge discloses that man has an existence within the world of spiritual beings, and that it is he himself who keeps within him his physical existence as a recollection. The question what after death will become of all that I now am, receives the following answer from clairvoyant investigation: "You will continue to be yourself just to that extent to which you realise that self to be a spiritual being amongst other spiritual beings."

We realise the nature of these spiritual beings and amongst them our own nature. And this knowledge is direct experience. Through it we know that spiritual beings, and with them our own soul, have an existence of which the physical existence is but a passing manifestation. If to ordinary consciousness it appears—as shown in the First Meditation—that the body belongs to a world whose real part in it is proved by its dissolution therein after death; clairvoyant observation teaches us that the real human ego belongs to a world to which it is attached by bonds quite different from those which connect the body with the laws of nature. The bonds which attach the ego to the spiritual beings of the supersensible world are not touched in their innermost character either by birth or by death. In physical existence these bonds only show themselves in a special way. That which appears in this world is the expression of realities of a supersensible nature. Now as man as such is a supersensible being, and also appears so to supersensible observation, so the bonds between souls in the supersensible world are not affected by death. And that anxious question which comes before the ordinary consciousness of the soul in this primitive form: "Shall I meet again after death those with whom I know I have been connected during physical existence?" must, by any real investigator, who is entitled to form a judgment based upon experience, be emphatically answered in the affirmative.

Everything that has been said of the being of the soul experiencing itself as a spiritual reality within the world of other spiritual beings, may be seen and confirmed if we only strengthen the life of our soul in the way mentioned before. And it is possible to make this easier and to help oneself along by the development of special feelings. In ordinary life in the physical world we take up such a position to all that we feel to be our fate, as to feel sympathy or antipathy for different occurrences. A self-observer, who is able to remain quite unbiased, must admit that these sympathies and antipathies are some of the strongest that man is able to feel. Ordinary reflection upon the fact that everything in life is a result of necessity, and that we have to bear our fate, may certainly take us a long way towards a deliberate attitude of mind in life. But in order to be able to grasp something of the real being of man still more is required. The reflection described will do excellent service in the life of our soul. We may, however, often find that those sympathies and antipathies of the kind mentioned, which we have been able to discard, have only disappeared from our immediate consciousness. They have retired into the deeper strata of human nature and manifest themselves as a certain mood of the soul or as a feeling of slackness or some other such sensation in the body. Real imperturbability with regard to fate is only acquired when we behave in this matter in just the same way as in the repeated concentrated surrender to thoughts or feelings for the purpose of strengthening the soul in general. A reflection only leading to intellectual understanding is not sufficient. It is necessary to live intensely with such a reflection, and to continue therein for a certain period of time while keeping away all experiences appertaining to the senses or other recollections of ordinary life. Through such exercises we arrive at a certain fundamental attitude of mind towards fate. It is possible radically to do away with sympathies and antipathies in this respect and finally to consider everything that happens to us quite as unconcernedly as an observer watches water falling over a mountainside and splashing down beneath. It is not meant that in this way we ought to arrive at facing our own fate without any feelings whatever. One who becomes indifferent to anything that happens to him is surely on no profitable track. We certainly do not remain indifferent to the outer world with regard to things not touching our own soul as part of our fate. We look upon things happening before our eyes with pleasure or with pain. Indifference to life should not be sought, when we strive after supersensible knowledge, but transformation of the direct interest that the ego takes in its own fate. It is quite possible that by such transformation the vividness of the life of feeling is strengthened and not weakened. In ordinary life tears are shed over many things that happen to our own soul in the way of fate. We are, however, able to win our way to a standpoint where the fate of others awakens in our soul the same keen interest and feeling as are induced by our own experiences. It is easier to arrive at such a standpoint with regard to our own mental capacities. It is not so easy, after all, to experience as great a joy when you discover a capacity in another, as when you discover that you possess that capacity yourself. When self-observation strives to penetrate into the depths of the soul, much selfish satisfaction with many things which we can do ourselves may be discovered. An intense, repeated meditative union with the thought, that in many instances it is quite indifferent to the course of human life whether we ourselves or others are able to do certain things, may carry us a long way towards true imperturbability with regard to that which we feel to be the innermost working of fate in our own lives. Such inner reinforcement of the life of our soul, by steeping it in thought, when rightly done, can never lead to a mere blunting of our feeling for our own capacities. Instead they are transformed and we realise the necessity of behaving in accordance with these capacities.

And here we have already indicated the direction taken by this strengthening of the life of the soul by thought. We learn to realise something in ourselves which appears to the soul as a second being within it. This becomes especially manifest, when we connect with it thoughts which show how in ordinary life we bring about this or that event in our destiny. We are able to see that this or that would not have happened to us, if we had not behaved in a certain way at an earlier period in our life. What

40

happens to us to-day is truly in many ways the result of what we did yesterday. We may now, with the intention of carrying our soul's experience further than some point at which we have arrived, look back upon our past experience. We may then search out all that shows how we ourselves have prepared our later destinies. We may try in so doing to go back so far as to reach that point where the consciousness awakens in the child, which enables it later in life to remember what it has experienced. If we set about this retrospect in such a way that we combine with it an attitude of mind which eliminates the usual selfish sympathies and antipathies with regard to occurrences in our own destiny, then, having reached in memory the above-mentioned point in our childhood, we face ourselves in such a way as to be able to say: At that time the possibility of feeling ourselves in ourselves and of conscious work upon the life of our soul first presented itself; but this ego of ours was there before, and it, although not working consciously within us, has brought us our capacity for knowledge as well as everything we now know. The attitude towards our own destiny just described brings about what no intellectual reflection is able to produce. We learn to look at the events of life with equanimity; we meet them with an unprejudiced mind; but we see in the being who brings these happenings upon us our own self. And when we look upon ourselves in this way, we find that the conditions of our own destiny, already given us at birth, are connected with our own self. We win our way to the conviction that just as we have worked upon ourselves since the awakening of our consciousness, so we had already been working before our present consciousness awoke. Now such a working of ourselves up to the realisation of a higher ego-being within the ordinary ego not only leads us to admit that our thoughts have brought us to a theoretical statement of the existence of such a higher ego, but also makes us realise as a power within ourselves the living activity of this ego in all its reality and feel the ordinary ego as a creation of the other. This feeling is, in fact, the first step towards beholding the spiritual being of the soul. And if it leads to nothing, it is because we rest satisfied with the beginning only. This beginning may be a scarcely perceptible dull sensation. It may remain so perhaps for a long time. But if we strongly and energetically pursue the course which has led us up to this beginning, we shall at last arrive at beholding the soul as a spiritual being. And having brought ourselves thus far we shall easily understand why some one, without any experience in these matters, may say that in believing we see such things we have only created an imaginative picture of a higher ego through auto-suggestion. But one who has had the experience knows that such an objection is only derived from lack of this very experience. For those who seriously go through this development acquire at the same time the capacity to distinguish between realities and the pictures of their own imagination. The inner activities and experiences which are necessary during such a pilgrimage of the soul, if it is a right one, make us practise the greatest circumspection towards ourselves with regard to imagination and reality. When we systematically strive to attain the experience of ourselves in the higher ego as spiritual beings, we shall consider as the principal experience that which is described at the beginning of this meditation and look upon the rest as a help to the soul on its pilgrimage.

SEVENTH MEDITATION

In which the Attempt is made to form an Idea of the Character of Experience in Supersensible Worlds

THE experiences that showed themselves to be necessary for the soul, if it wants to penetrate into supersensible worlds, may seem deterrent to many people. These may say they do not know what would befall them if they ventured upon such processes, or how they would be able to stand them. Under the influence of such a feeling the opinion is very easily formed that it is better not to interfere artificially with the development of the soul, but calmly to surrender to the guidance of which the soul remains unconscious, and to await its effect in the future upon the inner life of humanity. Such a thought must, however, always be repressed by a person who is able to make another thought a living power within him; namely, that it is natural to human nature to progress, and that if no attention were paid to these things it would mean disloyally consigning to stagnation forces in the soul which are waiting to be unfolded. Forces of self-unfolding are present in every human soul, and there cannot be a single one that would not listen to the call for unfolding them if in some way or other it could learn something about these powers and their importance.

Moreover, nobody will allow himself to be deterred from the ascent into higher worlds unless beforehand he has taken up a false position towards the processes through which he has to go.

These processes are described in the preceding meditations. And if they are to be expressed by words which must naturally be taken from ordinary human existence, they can be rightly expressed only in that way. For experiences on the supersensible path of knowledge are related to the human soul in such a way that they are exactly similar to what, for example, a highly-strung feeling of loneliness, a feeling of hovering over an abyss and the like may mean to the soul of man. Through the experience of such feelings and sensations the powers to tread the path of knowledge are produced. They are the germs of the fruits of supersensible knowledge. All these experiences in a certain way carry something in themselves which lies hidden deep within them. When they are experienced this hidden element is brought to a state of the utmost tension, something bursts the feeling of loneliness, which surrounds this hidden "something" like a veil, and it then pushes forward into the soul's life as a new means of knowledge.

One must, however, take into consideration that when the right path is entered upon, something else at once presents itself behind every such experience. When the one has occurred, the other cannot fail to appear. When anything has to be borne there is at once added the power to bear it steadfastly if we will only reflect calmly on this power and also take time to notice that which wants to manifest itself in the soul. When something painful appears, and when at the same time there is a sure feeling in the soul that forces are to be found which will make the pain bearable and with which we are able to connect ourselves, we are then able to take up such a position towards experiences, unbearable in the course of our ordinary life, so that we seem to be the spectator of ourselves in all such experiences. And thus people who, whilst on their way towards supersensible knowledge, pass through many a rise and fall of great waves of feeling, show nevertheless perfect equanimity in ordinary life. It is of course quite possible that experiences that are made within also react upon the state of mind in outer life in the physical world, so that for a time we do not come into harmony with ourselves and with life in the way which was possible before we entered upon the path of knowledge. We are

44

then obliged to draw from that which has already been obtained within ourselves such forces as make it possible again to find the balance. And if the path of knowledge be rightly trod no situation can arise in which this would not be possible.

The best path of knowledge will always be the one that leads to the supersensible world through strengthening or condensing the life of the soul by means of concentration on inner meditations during which certain thoughts or feelings are retained in the mind. In this case it is not a question of experiencing a thought or an emotion as we do in order to find our way in the physical world, but the point is to live entirely with and within the thought or emotion, concentrating all the powers of our soul in it, so that it entirely fills the consciousness during the time of retirement within ourselves. We think, for instance, of a thought which has given to the soul a conviction of some kind; we at first leave on one side any power of conviction it may have, and only live with it and in it again and again so as to become one with it. It is not necessary that it should be a thought of things belonging to the higher worlds, although such a thought is more effective. For inner meditation we can even use a thought which pictures an ordinary experience. Fruitful for instance, are emotions which represent resolutions with regard to deeds of love, and which we kindle within ourselves to the highest degree of human warmth and sincere experience. Effective—especially where knowledge is concerned—are symbolic representations, gained from life, or accepted on the advice of such persons as are in a certain way experts in these matters, because they know the fruitfulness of the means employed from what they themselves have gained by them.

Through these meditations, that must become a habit, nay, a necessity of life, just as breathing is necessary for the life of the body, we shall concentrate the powers of the soul, and by concentrating strengthen them. Only we must succeed during the time of inner meditation in remaining in such a state that neither outer impressions of the senses nor any recollections of such play upon the soul. Recollections also of all that we have experienced in ordinary life, all that gives pleasure or pain to the

45

soul, must remain silent so that the soul may surrender itself exclusively to that which we ourselves determine shall occupy it. The capacities for supersensible knowledge grow legitimately only out of that which we have acquired in this way by inner meditations, the content and the form of which have been fixed by the power of our own soul. The important point is not the source whence we derive the object of the meditation; we may take it from an expert in these matters or from the literature of spiritual science; the important point is to make its substance an inner experience of our own life and not merely to choose it out from thoughts which may arise in our own soul, or from things which we feel inclined to consider as the best objects for meditation. Such an object has but little power, because the soul is already familiar with it and cannot consequently make the necessary effort in order to become one with it. It is in making this effort, however, that the effective means of acquiring the faculties for supersensible knowledge are to be found, and not in the mere fact of becoming one with the substance of the meditation as such.

We can also arrive at supersensible sight in other ways. People may arrive at fervent meditation and inner experience by reason of their whole constitution. And so they may be able to liberate powers for acquiring supersensible knowledge in their soul. Such powers may all of a sudden manifest themselves in souls which do not seem at all predetermined for such experiences. In the most varied ways the supersensible life of the soul may awaken; but we can only arrive at an experience of which we are the masters as we are the masters of ourselves in ordinary life, if we tread the path of knowledge here described. Any other irruption of the supersensible world into the experiences of the soul will mean that such experiences enter in as it were forcibly, and the person in question will either lose himself in them, or lay himself open to every conceivable kind of deception with regard to their value, their true meaning, and their importance within the real supersensible world.

It is most important to keep in mind that on the path to supersensible knowledge the soul changes. It may be the case that in ordinary life in the physical world, we are not at all inclined to fall into any kind of illusion or deception, but that on entering the supersensible world we fall victims to such deceptions and illusions in the most credulous manner. It may also happen that in the physical world we have a very good and sound feeling for truth, and understand that we must not think only in such a way of a thing or an occurrence as to satisfy our own egoism in order to judge it rightly; yet in spite of this we may arrive at seeing only that in the supersensible world which pleases our egoism. We must remember how this egoism colours all that we behold. We are observing only that to which our egoism is directing its gaze in accordance with its own inclinations, though perhaps we may not realise that it is egoism which is directing our spiritual sight. And it is then quite natural that we should take what we see for truth. Protection against this can only be obtained if, on the path to supersensible knowledge through earnest self-observation, and through an energetic striving for clearer self-knowledge, we more and more develop our capacity to discern truly how much egoism is to be found in our own soul and where it is finding utterance. Only then we shall be able to emancipate ourselves by degrees from the leadership of this egoism if in our meditation we forcibly and relentlessly put before ourselves the possibility of our soul being in this or that respect under its domination.

It belongs to the unhampered mobility of the soul in higher worlds that it should make clear to itself in what a different manner certain qualities of the soul react upon the spiritual world from that in which they do in the physical world. This becomes especially evident when we direct our attention to the moral qualities of the soul. Within the physical world we distinguish between the laws of nature and those of morality. When we want to explain natural processes we cannot make use of moral ideas. We explain a poisonous plant according to natural law, and we do not condemn it morally for being poisonous. We clearly understand that, with regard to the animal kingdom, there can, at the most, be only a question of something resembling morality, and that a moral judgment in the strict sense could only disturb the main issue. It is in circumstances of human life that moral judgment about the worth of existence

47

begins to be of importance. Man himself makes his own value dependent on this judgment, when he comes so far that he is able to judge himself impartially. Nobody, however, would dream of considering the laws of nature as identical with or even similar to moral laws, if he considers physical existence in the right way.

As soon as we enter the higher worlds this is changed. The more spiritual the worlds which we enter, the more do moral law and what may be termed natural law in these worlds coincide. In the physical world we know that we are speaking figuratively when we say of an evil deed that it burns in the soul. We know that natural fire is quite a different thing. But such a distinction does not exist in the supersensible worlds; for there hate and envy are forces acting in such a way that we may term their effects the "natural laws" of that world. Hate and envy have there the effect that the being who is hated or envied reacts upon the hater or envier in a consuming, extinguishing manner, so that processes of destruction are established which are hurtful to the spiritual being. Love acts in such a way in spiritual worlds that its effect is an irradiation of warmth that is productive and helpful. This can already be observed in the elemental body of man. Within the sense-world the hand that commits an immoral action must in its activity be explained according to natural law quite in the same way as a hand that serves morality. But certain elemental parts of man remain undeveloped, when no corresponding moral feelings exist. And we must account for the imperfect formation of elemental organs through imperfect moral qualities in the same way as natural processes are explained by natural law. On the other hand, we must never from the imperfect development of a physical organ draw the conclusion that the corresponding part of the elemental body must be imperfectly developed. We must always keep in mind that in the different worlds different kinds of law prevail. A person may have a physical organ imperfectly developed; but at the same time the corresponding elemental organ may be not only normally perfect, but more perfect to the same extent as the physical one is imperfect.

In a significant way does the difference between the

supersensible and the physical worlds present itself in all that is connected with ideas of beauty and ugliness. The way in which these ideas are employed in physical existence loses all significance as soon as we enter supersensible worlds. Beautiful, for instance—only that being can be called beautiful which succeeds in communicating all its inner experiences to the other beings of its world, so that they can take part in the totality of its experience. The capacity of manifesting all that lives within oneself, and of not being compelled to hide away anything, might in higher worlds be called "beautiful." And in these worlds this conception of beauty completely coincides with that of unreserved sincerity, of honest manifestation of that which a being carries within itself. Similarly that being might be called ugly which does not want to show outwardly its own inner content, and which holds back its own experience and hides itself from other beings with regard to certain qualities. Such a feeing withdraws from its spiritual surroundings. This conception of ugliness coincides with that of insincere manifestation of oneself. To lie and to be ugly are realities which in the spiritual world are identical, so that a being which appears ugly is a deceitful being.

What are known in the physical world as desires and wishes also appear with quite a different significance in the spiritual world. Desires which in the physical world arise from the inner nature of the human soul do not exist in the spiritual world. What may be termed desires in that world are kindled by that which is seen outside the being in question. A being which must feel that it has not a certain quality, which, according to that being's nature, it should have, beholds another being endowed with that quality. Moreover it cannot help having this other being always before it. As in the physical world the eye naturally sees what is visible, so in the supersensible world the want of a quality always carries a being into the neighbourhood of another being endowed with the quality in question. And the sight of this other being becomes a continual reproach, that acts as a real force, making the being, who is hampered with the fault, desirous of amending it. This is quite different from a desire in the physical world; for in the spiritual world free will is

49

not interfered with through such circumstances. A being may oppose itself to that which the sight of something else will call forth within it. It will then succeed by degrees in being taken away from its model.

The consequence, however, will be that the being who opposes itself to its model will bring itself into worlds where the conditions of existence will be worse than those would have been which were given to it in the world for which it was in a certain way predestined.

All this shows the soul that its world of conceptions must be transformed when entering supersensible realms. Ideas must be changed, widened, and blended with others if we want to describe the supersensible world correctly. That is the reason why descriptions of supersensible worlds given in terms of the physical world without any alteration or transformation are always unsatisfactory. We may realise that it is the outcome of a correct human feeling, when we use, within the physical world —more or less symbolically or even as immediately applicable —ideas which only become fully significant with regard to supersensible worlds. Thus we may really feel lying to be ugly, but compared with the character of this idea in the supersensible world, such a use of words in the physical world is only a reflection, resulting from the fact that all the different worlds are related to one another, and these relations are dimly felt and unconsciously perceived in the physical world. Yet we must remember that in the physical world a lie, which we feel as ugly, is not necessarily ugly in its outer appearance, and that it would be a confusion of ideas if we were to explain ugliness in physical nature as the outcome of lying. In the supersensible world, however, anything false, seen in its right light, impresses itself upon us as being ugly in appearance. Here again possible deceptions have to be taken into consideration and guarded against. The soul may meet a being in the supersensible world which may rightly be characterised as evil, although it manifests itself in a form that must be called beautiful if judged according to the idea of the beautiful that we bring with us from the physical world. In such a case we shall not be able to judge correctly before we have penetrated to the heart of the being in

question. We shall then discover that the "beautiful"
manifestation was only a mask which does not harmonise with
the nature of the being, and then that which we thought to be
beautiful—according to ideas borrowed from the physical world
—impresses itself with particular force upon our mind as ugly.
And as soon as this happens, the "evil" being will no more be
able to deceive us with its "beauty." It must unveil itself to such
a beholder in its true form, which can only be an imperfect
expression of that which it is within. Such phenomena of the
supersensible world make it especially evident how human
conceptions must be transformed when we enter that world.

EIGHTH MEDITATION

In which the Attempt is made to form an Idea of the Way in which Man beholds his Repeated Earth-Lives

WE are not really entitled to speak of dangers during the pilgrimage of the soul through supersensible worlds, when this pilgrimage is undertaken in the right way. The method would not lead to its goal if amongst the psychic instructions given there were those which created dangers for the pupil. The goal is rather to make the soul strong, to concentrate its forces, so that man should become able to bear his soul's experiences, which he has to go through when he wants to see and understand other worlds than the physical. Moreover, an essential difference between the physical world and the supersensible worlds is that beholding, perceiving, and understanding are related to one another in quite a different way in the two worlds. When we hear about some part of the physical world, we have a certain right to feel that we can only arrive at a complete understanding thereof through beholding and perceiving it. We do not believe we have understood a landscape or a picture until we have seen it. But the supersensible worlds can be thoroughly understood when with unbiased judgment we accept a correct description of them. In order to understand and to experience all the forces for the strengthening and fulfilment of life which belong to spiritual worlds, we only need the descriptions of those who are able to see. Real knowledge of those worlds at first hand can only be obtained by those who are able to investigate when outside their physical body. Descriptions of the spiritual worlds must always originate with the seers. But such knowledge of these worlds as is necessary to the life of the soul may be obtained through the understanding alone. And it is perfectly possible to be unable to look into supersensible worlds oneself and yet be able to understand them and their peculiarities, with an understanding for which the soul has under certain circumstances a perfect right to ask, and indeed must ask.

Therefore it is also possible that we should choose our means of meditation out of the store of conceptions which we have acquired concerning the spiritual worlds. Such a means of meditation is by far the best and the one which leads us most safely to the goal.

Although such a notion may seem very natural, it is, however, not correct to believe that knowledge of higher worlds obtained through the understanding before attaining to supersensible vision is an obstacle to the development of such vision. The contrary is in fact more correct, namely, that it is easier and safer to strive for clairvoyance with some preliminary understanding than without. Whether we stop short at understanding only, or go on to strive after clairvoyance, depends upon the awakening or non-awakening of an inner craving for first-hand knowledge. If such a craving is there, we cannot but look for every opportunity to start on a real personal pilgrimage into supersensible worlds.

The wish for an understanding of the higher worlds will spread more and more amongst the people of our day; for close observation of human evolution shows that from now onward human souls are entering upon a stage of development in which they will be unable to find the right relation to life without an understanding of supersensible worlds.

* * * * *

When we have come so far on our psychic pilgrimage that we carry within ourselves as a memory all that we call "ourself," namely, our own being in physical life, and experience ourselves instead in another, newly-won superior ego, then we

53

become capable of seeing our life stretching beyond the limits of earthly life. Before our spiritual sight appears the fact that we have shared in another life, in the spiritual world, prior to our present existence in the world of the senses; and in that spiritual life are to be found the real causes of the shaping of our physical existence. We become acquainted with the fact that before we received a physical body and entered upon this physical existence we lived a purely spiritual life. We see that that human being which we now are, with its faculties and inclinations, was prepared during a life that we spent in a purely spiritual world before birth. We look upon ourselves as upon beings who lived spiritually before their entrance into the world of the senses, and who are now striving to live as physical beings with those faculties and psychic characteristics which were originally attached to them and which have developed since their birth. It would be a mistake to say: "How is it possible that in spiritual life I should have aspired to possess faculties and inclinations, which now, when I have got them, do not please me at all?" It does not matter, whether something pleases the soul in the world of senses or not. That is not the point. The soul has quite different points of view for its aspirations in the spiritual world from those which it adopts in the life of the senses. The character of wisdom and will is quite different in the two worlds. In the spiritual life we know that for the sake of our total evolution we need a certain kind of life in the physical world, which when we get there may seem unsympathetic or depressing to the soul; and yet we strive for it, because in the spiritual existence we do not prefer what is sympathetic and agreeable, but what is necessary to the right development of our individual being.

It is the same with regard to the events of life. We contemplate them and see how we have prepared in the spiritual world what is antipathetic as well as what is sympathetic, and how we ourselves have brought together the impulses which cause our painful as well as our joyful experiences in physical existence. But even then we may find it incomprehensible that we ourselves have brought about this or that situation in life, as long as we only experience ourselves in the physical world. In the spiritual world, however, we have had what may be called supersensible insight which caused us to say: "You must go through that uncongenial or painful experience, for only such an experience can bring you a step further in your total development." From the standpoint of the physical world only, it is never possible to decide how far one particular life on earth brings a human being forward in his total evolution.

Having realised the spiritual existence that precedes our earthly existence, we see the reasons why in our spiritual life we have aimed at a certain kind of destiny for the ensuing terrestrial life. These reasons lead back to an earlier terrestrial life lived in the past. Upon the character of that earlier life, upon the experiences made and the capacities attained therein, depends the wish during the succeeding spiritual existence to correct defective experiences and develop neglected capacities through a new life upon earth. In the spiritual world you feel a wrong done by you to another human being to be a disturbance of the harmony of the world, and you realise the necessity of meeting that human being again on earth in the next terrestrial life, in order to be able to get into such relationship to him as to be able to repair the wrong you have done. During the progressive development of the soul the range of vision is widened over a whole series of earlier terrestrial lives. In this way you arrive through observation at a knowledge of the true history of the life of your higher "Ego." You see that man goes through his total existence in a succession of lives upon earth, and that between these repeated terrestrial lives he passes through purely spiritual states of existence which are connected with his terrestrial lives according to certain laws.

Thus the knowledge of repeated existences upon earth is lifted into the sphere of observation. (In order to avoid a frequently repeated mistake, attention is called to the following fact, more fully treated in other writings of mine. The sum total of a man's existence does not unfold itself in an endless repetition of lives. A certain number of repetitions take place, but both before the beginning and after the close of these quite different kinds of existence are found, and all this shows itself in its totality as a development inspired by sublime wisdom.)

The knowledge of repeated terrestrial lives may also be reached by reasonable observation of physical existence. In my books Theosophy and An Outline of Occult Science, as well as in lesser writings of mine, the attempt has been made to prove reincarnation along such lines of reasoning as are characteristic of the modern doctrine of evolution in natural science. It is there shown how logical thought and investigation that really follow out scientific research (and its results) to its full consequences are absolutely bound to accept the idea of evolution, presented to us by modern science, in such a sense as to consider the true being, the psychic individuality of man, as something which is evolving through a sequence of physical existences alternating with intermediate purely spiritual lives. The proofs attempted in those writings are naturally capable of much further development and completion. But the opinion does not seem unjustified that proofs in this matter have precisely the same scientific value as that which in general is called scientific proof. There is nothing in the science of spiritual things which cannot be confirmed by proofs of that kind. But of course we must admit the difficulty is greater for spiritually scientific proofs to be acknowledged than proofs of natural science. This is not on account of their less stringent logic, but because in the face of such proofs one does not feel those underlying physical facts, which make the acceptance of the proofs of natural science so easy. This has nothing whatever to do with the conclusiveness of the reasoning itself. And if we are capable of comparing with an unbiased mind the proofs of natural science with those given on analogous lines by spiritual science, we shall easily be convinced of their equally conclusive power. Thus the force of such proofs may also be added to that which the investigator of the spiritual worlds has to give as a description of successive terrestrial lives resulting from his own vision. The one side can support the other in the formation of a conviction of the truth of human reincarnation based simply on reasonable comprehension. Here the attempt has been made to show the way that leads beyond mental comprehension to supersensible vision of this reincarnation.

The Threshold of the
Spiritual World

INTRODUCTORY REMARKS

IN this book there are given in an aphoristic form some descriptions of those parts of the universe and of the human being which come into view when spiritual knowledge crosses the boundary between the physical and spiritual worlds. It has not been sought to give either a systematic or in any way a complete account, but merely a few descriptions of spiritual experiences without any fixed plan. In this respect the present work, like my book, A Road to Self-Knowledge (published with this), is intended to complete and amplify my other writings. Yet it has also been sought to give the description in such a way that it may be read independently, without any knowledge of these other works.

One who really means to work his way to a knowledge of spiritual science will feel the necessity of continually contemplating the spiritual side of life from continually fresh points of view. It is indeed only natural that a certain one-sidedness should be connected with every presentation of this kind. This must be the case much more with descriptions of the spiritual sphere than with those of the physical world. And if we rest satisfied with merely one account, we cannot be said to be pursuing spiritual knowledge seriously. My desire, by such writings as this, is to be of use to those who are really in earnest in seeking knowledge of the spiritual world. On this account I try to present spiritual facts again and again from fresh points of view in spite of my having described them from other points of view in other works. Such accounts are complementary of each other, like photographs of a person or an event taken from various points.

In every such description, made from a certain standpoint, there is an opportunity for communicating knowledge which is not attainable from the other points of view. There are again in this book formulae for meditation for those who are seeking spiritual sight for themselves. Those who are looking for such formulae wherewith to develop the life of their soul will easily find them here.

RUDOLF STEINER.

August 1913.

The Threshold of the Spiritual World

I

Concerning the Reliance which may be placed on Thinking; the Nature of the Thinking Soul; and of Meditation

IN waking consciousness human thought is like an island in the midst of the stream of the soul's life, which flows by in impressions, sensations, feelings, and so forth. We have to a certain degree finished with an impression or a sensation when we have formed an idea concerning it, that is, when we have framed a thought which throws light on the impression or sensation. Even in a storm of passion and emotion, a certain degree of calm may set in, if the ship of the soul has worked its way to the island of thought.

The soul has a natural confidence in thinking. It feels that if it could not have this confidence, all stability in life would be lost. The healthy life of the soul comes to an end when it begins to doubt about thinking. For even if we cannot arrive at a clear understanding of something through thought, we may yet have the consolation that clearness would result if we could only rouse ourselves to think with sufficient force and acuteness. We

can reassure ourselves with regard to our own incapacity to clear
up a point by thinking; but the thought is intolerable that
thinking itself would not be able to bring satisfaction, even if we
were to penetrate as far into its domain as was necessary for
gaining full light on some definite situation in life.

This attitude of the soul with regard to thinking underlies all
human efforts after knowledge. It may be dulled in certain
moods of the soul, but it is always to be found in the soul's dim
feelings. The thinker who doubts the validity and power of
thought itself is deceived about the fundamental state of his
soul. For it is often really his acuteness of thought which, being
overstrained, constructs doubts and perplexities. If he did not
really rely on thinking, he would not be tormented with these
doubts, which after all are only the result of thinking.

One who develops in himself the feeling here indicated with
regard to thought, feels that the latter is not merely something
which he is cultivating in himself as a human force of the soul,
but also something which quite independently of him and his
soul bears within itself some Being of a cosmic nature, a Being
to whom he must work his way, if he intends to live in
something which belongs at the same time to him and to the
world that is independent of him.

There is something deeply tranquillising in being able to
surrender oneself to the life of thought. The soul feels that in
that life it can escape from itself. This feeling is as necessary to
the soul as the opposite one of being able to be wholly within
itself.

In the necessary change between these two conditions lies the
healthy rhythm of the soul's life. Waking and sleeping are really
only the extremes of these conditions. When awake the soul is in
itself, living its own life; in sleep it loses itself in the universal
life of the world, and is therefore to a certain extent freed from
itself. The conditions in either direction correspond to the
various inner experiences. And the life of thought is a release of
the soul from itself, just as feeling, sensation, emotional life, and
so forth are the expression of the soul remaining within itself.

Looked at in this way, thought offers to the soul the
consolation which it needs when face to face with the feeling of

utter loneliness in the world. It is possible to arrive in quite a legitimate way at the feeling, "What am I in the current of universal cosmic events, flowing from one infinity to another—I with my feelings, desires, and will which surely can be of importance to me only?" Directly the life of thought has been rightly realised, this feeling is confronted by another. "The thought which is concerned with these cosmic events draws into itself me and my soul; I am living in those events when I, through thinking, let their being flow into me." It is then possible to feel oneself taken into the universe and secure therein. From this condition of the soul, a strength ensues, which feels as though it had come from the cosmic powers themselves, in accordance with wise laws.

It is but another step from this feeling to that in which the soul says, "It is not only I who think, but something thinks in me; the cosmic life expresses itself in me; my soul is only the stage upon which the universe manifests itself as thought."

This feeling may be repudiated by this or that philosophy. It may, with various reasons, be made apparently quite obvious that the thought which has just been expressed, of the world thinking itself in the human soul, is entirely erroneous. In answer to this it must be realised that this thought is one which can be worked out through inner experience. Only one who has thus worked it out fully understands its validity, and knows that no refutations can shake that validity. One who has thus mastered it sees from this very thought, quite clearly, what so many refutations and proofs are really worth. They may appear infallible when you still erroneously believe in the convincing power of their content. In that case it is difficult to come to an understanding with people who consider such proofs as conclusive. They are bound to think another person mistaken, because they have not yet accomplished the inner work within themselves which has brought him to a recognition of what seems to them erroneous, or perhaps even absurd.

For one who wishes to find his way into spiritual science, meditations such as the foregoing on thinking are of benefit. For such a person it is a question of bringing his soul into a condition which gives it access to the spiritual world. Access may be denied to the clearest thinking or to the most perfect scientific method, if the soul does not bring anything to meet the spiritual facts, or the information about them ready to press in upon it. It may be a good preparation for the apprehension of spiritual knowledge to have felt frequently what invigorating force tnere is in the attitude of soul which says, "I feel myself to be one in thought with the stream of cosmic events." In this case it is less a question of the abstract value of this thought as knowledge, than of having often felt in our souls the powerful effect which is experienced when such a thought flows with force through the inner life and circulates like a breath of spiritual oxygen through the soul. It is not only a question of recognising what there is in a thought of this kind, but of experiencing it. The thought is recognised when once it has been present in the soul with sufficient power of conviction; but if it is to ripen and bear fruit which shall promote understanding of the spiritual world, its beings and facts, it must, after having been understood, be made to live in the soul again and again. The soul must again and again be filled with the thought, allowing nothing else to be present in it, and shutting out all other thoughts, feelings, memories, and so forth. Repeated concentration of this kind on such a thoroughly grasped thought draws together forces in the soul which in ordinary life are to some extent dissipated. The soul concentrates and strengthens these forces within itself, and they become the organs for the perception of the spiritual world and its truths.

The right way in which to meditate may be learned from what has just been pointed out. We first work our way through to a thought which may be realised with the means that lie ready to hand in ordinary life and knowledge. Then we plunge into that thought again and again, and make ourselves completely one with it. The strengthening of the soul is the result of living with a thought which has thus been recognised. In this case the above thought was chosen as an example which was derived from the very nature of thinking. It was chosen as an example because it is very specially fruitful for meditation. But what has been said here holds good, with regard to meditation, for every thought which is acquired in the way that has been described. It is especially fruitful for meditation when we know the state of soul which results from the above-mentioned rhythmic swing in the life of the soul. By that means we arrive in the surest way at the feeling of having been in direct touch with the spiritual world during our meditation.

And this feeling is a sound result of meditation. The force of it should give strength to the rest of our daily life, and not in such a way that an ever-present impression of the meditative state is present the whole time, but so that one feels that from the meditative experience strength is flowing into our whole life.

If the state brought about by meditation extends through daily life as an ever-present impression, it diffuses something which disturbs the mental ease of that life. And the state of meditation itself will not then be sufficiently pure and strong. Meditation gives the best results when through its own character it is kept apart from ordinary life. It influences life in the best way when it is felt to be something distinct from and raised above ordinary life.

II

Concerning Knowledge of the Spiritual World

COMPREHENSION of the facts stated by spiritual science is made easier, if in the ordinary life of the soul attention be given to that which gives rise to ideas capable of such enlargement and transformation that they gradually reach as far as the events and beings of the spiritual world. And unless this path be followed with patience we shall easily be tempted to picture the spiritual world too much like the physical world of the senses. Indeed, unless we follow this path we shall not be able to form a just conception of what is actually spiritual, and of its relation to man.

Spiritual events and beings crowd in upon man when he has prepared his soul to perceive them. The way in which they announce themselves is absolutely different from the way in which physical beings and facts do so. But an idea of this entirely different way of manifesting may be gained if the process of remembering be called to mind. Let us suppose we had an experience some time ago. At a definite moment—from one cause or another—this experience emerges from the depths of psychic life. We know that what so emerges corresponds to an experience, and we relate it to that experience. But at the moment of remembrance there is nothing of the experience present but only its image in the memory. Now let us imagine an image rising up in the soul in the same way as does a picture of memory yet expressing, not something previously experienced

65

but something unfamiliar to the soul. If we do this, we have formed an idea of the way in which the spiritual world first makes its appearance in the soul, when the latter is sufficiently prepared for it.

Because this is so, one who is not sufficiently conversant with the conditions of the spiritual world will be perpetually bringing forward the objection that all "presumed" spiritual experiences are nothing else than more or less indistinct images of the memory, and that the soul merely does not recognise them as such and therefore takes them to be manifestations of a spiritual world. Now it should on no account be denied that it is difficult to distinguish between illusions and realities in this sphere. Many people who believe they have manifestations from a spiritual world are certainly only occupied with their own memories, which they do not recognise as such. In order to see quite clearly in this respect, it is necessary to be informed of those numerous sources from which illusion may arise. We may have seen, for instance, something only once and for a moment, seen it so hastily that the impression did not penetrate completely into the consciousness; and later—perhaps in a quite different form—it may appear as a vivid picture. We possibly feel convinced that we never had anything to do with the matter before, and that we have had a genuine inspiration.

This and many other things make it quite comprehensible that the statements made by those who have supersensible sight appear extremely questionable to those unacquainted with the special nature of spiritual science. But one who pays careful heed to all that is said in my books, The Way of Initiation and Initiation and its Results, about the development of spiritual sight, will be put in the way of being able to distinguish between illusion and truth in this sphere.

In this connection, however, the following should also be noted. It is true that spiritual experiences appear in the first place as pictures. It is thus that they rise out of the depths of the soul that is prepared for them. It is then a question of gaining the right relation to these pictures. They only have value for supersensible perception when, by the way in which they present themselves, they show that they are not to be taken for the facts themselves. Directly they are so taken, they are worth little more than ordinary dreams. They must present themselves to us like the letters of an alphabet. We do not look at the shape of the letters, but read in them what it is desired to express by their means. Just as something written does not call upon us to describe the form of the letters, so the images forming the content of supersensible sight do not call upon us to apprehend them as anything but images; but by their own character they force us to look right through their pictured form and direct our soul's gaze to that which, as a supersensible event or being, is endeavouring to express itself through them.

As little as a person on hearing that a letter contains news previously unknown can deny the possibility of this fact on account of the well-known character of the letters of the alphabet of which it is composed, so little can anybody object to clairvoyant pictures being formed out of well-known objects taken from ordinary life.

It is certainly true, up to a certain point, that the pictures are borrowed from ordinary life, but what is so borrowed is not the important thing to genuine clairvoyant consciousness. The important point is what lies behind and expresses itself through the pictures.

The soul must, of course, first prepare itself for seeing such images appear within its spiritual horizon; but, besides this, it must carefully cultivate the feeling of not stopping short at merely seeing them, but of relating them in the right way to the facts of the supersensible world. It may be said positively that for true clairvoyance there is required not only the capacity for beholding a world of images in oneself, but another faculty as well, which may be compared with reading in the physical world.

The supersensible world is at first to be looked upon as something lying wholly outside man's ordinary consciousness, which has no means of penetrating into that world. The powers of the soul, strengthened by meditation, first bring it into contact with the supersensible world. By means of these the pictures that have been described emerge from the wave of the soul's life. As pictures these are woven entirely by the soul itself. And the materials of which they are made are actually the forces which the soul has acquired for itself in the physical world. The fabric of the pictures is really nothing else but what may be characterised as memory. The clearer we make this to ourselves, in order to understand clairvoyant consciousness, the better. We shall in that case clearly understand that they are but images. And we shall also be cultivating a right understanding of the way in which the images are to be related to the supersensible world. Through the pictures we shall learn to read in the supersensible world. The impressions of the physical world naturally bring us much nearer to the beings and events of that world than the images seen supersensibly bring us to the supersensible world. We might even say that these images are at first like a curtain put up by the soul between it and the supersensible world, when it feels itself to be in contact with that world.

It is a question of becoming gradually familiar with the way in which supersensible things are experienced. Through experience we learn by degrees to read the images, that is, to interpret them correctly. In more important supersensible experiences, their very nature shows that we cannot here have to do with mere pictures of memory from ordinary life. It is indeed true that in this connection many absurd things are asserted by people who have been convinced of certain supersensible facts, or at any rate think they have been. Many people, for instance, when convinced of the truth of reincarnation, at once connect the pictures which arise in their soul with experiences of a former earth-life; but one should always be suspicious when these pictures seem to point to previous earth-lives which are similar in one respect or another to the present one, or which make their appearance in such a way that the present life can, by reasoning, be plausibly explained from the supposed earlier lives. When, in the course of genuine supersensible experience, the true impression of a former earth-life, or of several such lives, appears, it generally happens that the former life or lives are such that we could never have fashioned them or have desired to fashion them in thought by any amount of thinking back from the present life, or out of any wishes and efforts in

connection with it. We may, for instance, receive an impression
of our former earth existence at some moment during our
present life when it is quite impossible to acquire certain
faculties, which we had during that former life. So far from its
being the case that images appear for the more important
spiritual experiences which might be memories of ordinary life,
the pictures for these are generally such as we should not have
thought of at all in ordinary experience. This tendency increases
with real impressions the more purely supersensible the worlds
become from which they issue. Thus it is often quite impossible
to form images from ordinary life explanatory of the existence
between birth and the preceding death. We may find out that in
the spiritual life we have developed affection for people and
things in complete contrast with the corresponding inclinations
we are developing in the present life on earth; and we learn that
in our earth-life we have often been driven to be fond of
something which in the previous spiritual existence (between
death and rebirth) we have rejected and avoided. Any memory
of this existence which might be imagined to result from
ordinary physical experiences must therefore necessarily be
different from the impression we receive through real perception
in the spiritual world.

One who is not familiar with spiritual science will certainly
make further objections against things being in reality as they
have just been described. He will be able to say, for instance:
"You are indeed fond of something, but human nature is
complicated, and secret antipathy is mixed up with every
affection. This antipathy to the thing referred to comes up in you
at a particular moment. You think it is a prenatal experience,
whereas it may perhaps be quite naturally explained from the
subconscious psychic facts of the case." In general there is
nothing to be said against such an objection; and in many cases
it may be quite correct. Knowledge of clairvoyant consciousness
is not easily gained, nor is it without the possibility of
objections. But just as it is true that a supposed clairvoyant may
be mistaken and regard a subconscious fact as an experience of
prenatal spirit-life, so it is also true that a training in spiritual
science leads to a knowledge of self which embraces

subconscious states of soul and is able to free itself from any illusions with regard to them. Here it need only be asserted that that supersensible knowledge alone is true which at the moment of cognition is able to distinguish what originates from supersensible worlds from that which has merely been shaped by individual imagination. This faculty of discernment becomes so developed by familiarity with supersensible worlds, that perception may in this sphere be as certainly distinguished from imagination, as in the physical world hot iron which is touched with the finger may be distinguished from imaginary hot iron.

III

Concerning Man's Etheric Body and the Elemental World

MAN arrives at the recognition and knowledge of a supersensible spiritual world by overcoming certain obstacles in the way of such a recognition, which at the outset are present in his soul. The difficulty in this case is due to the fact that these obstacles, though affecting the course of the soul's inner experience, are not apprehended as such by ordinary consciousness. For there are many things present, and living, in the human soul, of which at first it knows nothing, and of which it has to gain knowledge by degrees, just as it does of beings and events belonging to the outer world.

The spiritual world, before it is perceived and recognised by the soul, is to the latter something quite strange and unfamiliar, the qualities of which have nothing in common with what the soul is able to learn through its experiences in the physical world. Thus it comes about that the soul may be confronted with the spiritual world and may see in it an absolute void. The soul may feel as though it were looking into an infinite, blank, desolate abyss. Now this feeling actually exists in those depths of the soul of which it is at first unconscious. The feeling is something like fear and dread, and the soul lives in it without being aware of the fact. For the life of the soul is determined not only by what it knows, but by that which is actually present within it, without its knowledge. Now when the soul searches, in

the sphere of thought, for reasons for disproving and for
evidence against the spiritual world, it does so, not because
those reasons are conclusive in themselves, but because it is
seeking for a kind of narcotic to dull the feeling just described.
People do not deny the existence of the spiritual world, or the
possibility of attaining knowledge of it, as a result of being able
to prove its non-existence, but because they desire to fill their
souls with thoughts which will deceive them and rid them of
their dread of the spiritual world. Liberation from this longing
for a materialistic narcotic for deadening the dread of the
spiritual world cannot be gained till a survey is made of the
whole circumstances of this part of the soul's life, as here
described. "Materialism as a psychic phenomenon of fear" is an
important chapter in the science of the soul.

This dread of the spiritual becomes intelligible when we have
won our way through to a recognition of the spiritual; when we
have come to see that the events and beings of the physical
world are the outward expression of supersensible, spiritual
events and beings. We arrive at this understanding when we can
see that the body belonging to man, which is perceptible to the
senses and with which alone ordinary science is concerned, is
the expression of a subtle, supersensible, or etheric body, in
which the material or physical body is enclosed, like a denser
nucleus, as though in a cloud.

This etheric body is the second principle of human nature. It
forms the basis of the life of the physical body. But as regards
his etheric body man is not cut off from its corresponding outer
world to the same extent to which his physical body is detached
from the physical outer world. When we speak of an outer world
in connection with the etheric body, it is not the physical outer
world, perceived by the senses, that is meant, but a spiritual
environment which is as supersensible in relation to the physical
world as man's etheric body is in relation to his physical body.
Man, as an etheric being, stands in an etheric, or elemental
world.

Man is always "experiencing" the fact, although in ordinary
life he knows nothing of it, that he, as an etheric being, inhabits
an elemental world. When he becomes conscious of this state of

things, the consciousness is quite different from that of ordinary experience. This new consciousness sets in when man becomes clairvoyant. The clairvoyant then knows about that which is always present in life, though hidden from ordinary consciousness.

Now in his ordinary consciousness man calls himself "I," signifying the being which presents itself in his physical body. The healthy life of his soul in the world of the senses depends on his thus recognising himself as a being separated from the rest of the world. That healthy psychic life would be interrupted if he characterised any other events or beings of the outer world as part of his ego. When man realises himself as an etheric being in the elemental world, things are different. Then his own ego-being blends with certain occurrences and beings around him. The etheric human being has to find himself in that which is not his inner being, in the same sense as "inner" is conceived in the physical world. In the elemental world there are forces, occurrences, and beings which, although in certain respects part of the outer world, must yet be considered as belonging to one's own ego. As etheric human beings we are woven into the elemental essence of the world. In the physical world we have our thoughts, with which we are so bound up that we may look upon them as forming a constituent part of our ego. But there are forces, occurrences, and so forth which act as intimately upon the inner nature of the etheric human being as thoughts do in the physical world; and which do not behave like thoughts, but are like beings living with and in the soul. Therefore clairvoyance needs a stronger inner force than that which the soul possesses for the purpose of maintaining its own independence in the face of its thoughts. And the essential preparation for true clairvoyance consists in so strengthening and invigorating the soul inwardly, that it can be conscious of itself as an individual being, not only in the presence of its own thoughts, but also when the forces and beings of the elemental world enter the field of its consciousness as if they were a part of its own being.

Now that force of the soul by means of which it maintains its position as a being in the elemental world, is present in man's ordinary life. The soul at first knows nothing of this force, although possessing it. In order to possess it consciously, the soul must first prepare itself. It must acquire that inner force of the soul which is gained during the preparation for clairvoyance. As long as a man cannot make up his mind to acquire this inner force, he has a quite comprehensible dread of recognising his spiritual environment, and he—unconsciously—has recourse to the illusion that the spiritual world does not exist or cannot be known. This illusion delivers him from his instinctive dread of the growing together or blending of his own individual essence, or ego-being, with an actual outer spiritual world.

One who sees into the facts which have been described, comes to recognise an etheric human being behind the physical human being, and a supersensible, etheric, or elemental world behind the one that is physically perceptible.

Clairvoyant consciousness finds in the elemental world real beings which up to a certain point have independence, just as physical consciousness finds thoughts in the physical world which are unreal and have no independence. Growing familiarity with the elemental world leads to seeing these partially independent beings in closer connection with each other. Just as someone may first look upon the limbs of a physical human body as partially independent, and afterwards acknowledge them to be parts of the body as a whole, so to clairvoyant consciousness are the several beings of the elemental world embraced within one great spiritual body, of which they are living members. In the further course of clairvoyant experience that body comes to be recognised as the elemental, supersensible, etheric body of the earth. Within the earth's etheric body an etheric human being feels himself to be a member of a whole.

This progress in clairvoyance is a process of growing familiar with the nature of the elemental world. That world is inhabited by beings of the most widely different kinds. If we desire to express the activity of these force-beings, we can only do it by portraying their various peculiarities in pictures. Amongst them are beings which are found to be allied with everything which makes for endurance, solidity, and weight. They may be

74

designated as earth-souls. (And if we do not think ourselves overwise, and are not afraid of an image which only points to reality and is not reality itself, we may speak of them as Gnomes.) We also find beings which are so constituted that they may be designated as air, water, and fire souls.

Then again other beings appear. It is true that they so manifest themselves that they seem to be elemental or etheric beings, yet it may be seen that there is something in their etheric nature which is of higher quality than the essence of the elemental world. We learn to understand that it is as impossible to apprehend the real nature of these beings with the degree of clairvoyance sufficient only for the elemental world, as it is to arrive at the true nature of man with merely physical consciousness.

The beings mentioned above, which may figuratively be called earth, water, air, and fire souls, are, with the activity proper to them, situated in a certain respect within the earth's elemental etheric body. Their tasks lie there. But the beings of a higher nature which have been characterised carry their activity beyond the earth-sphere. If we come to know them better, through clairvoyant experience, we ourselves and our consciousness are carried in the spirit beyond the sphere of earth. We see how this earth-sphere has been developed from another, and how it is evolving within itself spiritual germs so that in time to come a further sphere, in a sense of a new earth, may arise out of it. My book Occult Science explains why that from which the earth was formed may be designated as an "old Moon-planet," and why the world towards which the earth aspires in the future may be called Jupiter. The essential point is that by the "old Moon," we understand a world long gone by, from which the earth has formed itself by transformation; whilst we understand Jupiter, in a spiritual sense, to be a future world, towards which the earth is aspiring.

IV

Summary of the Foregoing

UNDERLYING man's physical being is a subtle, etheric human being which lives in an elemental environment, as physical man lives in a physical environment. The elemental outer world is incorporated in the supersensible etheric body of the earth. This latter proves to be the transmuted essence of an earlier or Moon-world, and the preparatory stage of a future world (Jupiter). One may give the foregoing schematically as follows. Man contains:
—

I. The physical body, in the surrounding physical, material world. Through this body, man comes to recognise himself as an independent, individual being, or ego.

II. The subtle, etheric body in the surrounding elemental world. By its means man comes to recognise himself as a member of the earth's etheric body, and hence indirectly as a member of it in three consecutive planetary conditions.

V

Concerning Reincarnation and Karma; Man's Astral Body and the Spiritual World; and Ahrimanic Beings

IT is especially difficult for the soul to recognise that there is something prevailing within its life which is environment to the soul in the same way as the so-called outer world is environment to the ordinary senses. The soul unconsciously resists this, because it imagines its independent existence imperilled by such a fact; and therefore instinctively turns away from it. For though more modern science theoretically admits the existence of the fact, this does not mean that it is as yet fully realised, with all the consequences of inwardly grasping it and becoming permeated with it. If, however, our consciousness can attain to realising it as a vital fact, we learn to discern in the soul's nature an inner nucleus, which exists independently of everything that may be developed in the sphere of the soul's conscious life between birth and death. We learn to know in our own depths a being of which we feel our own self to be the creation, and by which we also feel that our body, the vehicle of consciousness, has been created, with all its powers and attributes.

In the course of this experience the soul learns to feel that a spiritual entity within it is growing to maturity, and that this entity withdraws itself from the influence of conscious life. It begins to feel that this inner entity becomes more and more vigorous, and also more independent, in the course of the life between birth and death. It learns to realise that the entity bears the same relation to the rest of experience, between birth and death, as the developing germ in the being of a plant bears to the sum-total of the plant in which it is developing: with the difference that the germ of the plant is of a physical, whilst the germ of the soul is of a spiritual nature.

The course of such an experience leads one to admit the idea of repeated earthly lives. In the nucleus of the soul, which is to a certain degree independent of the soul, the latter is able to feel the germ of a new human life. Into that life the germ will carry over the results of the present one, when it has experienced in a spiritual world after death, in a purely spiritual way, those conditions of life in which it cannot share as long as it is enveloped in a physical earthly body between birth and death.

From this thought there necessarily results another, namely, that the present physical life between birth and death is the product of other lives long past, in which the soul developed a germ which continued to live on in a purely spiritual world after death, till it was ripe for entering upon a new earthly life through a new birth; just as the germ of the plant becomes a new plant when, after having been detached from the old plant in which it was formed, it has been for a while in other conditions of life.

When the soul has been adequately prepared, clairvoyant consciousness learns to immerse itself in the process of the development in one human life of a germ, in a certain way independent, which carries over the results of that life into later earthly lives. In the form of a picture, yet essentially real, as though it were about to reveal itself as an individual entity, there emerges from the waves of the life of the soul a second self, which appears independent of and set over the being which we have previously looked upon as ourself. It seems like an inspirer of that self. And we as this latter self, then flow into one with our inspiring, superior self.

Now our ordinary consciousness lives in this state of things, which is thus beheld by clairvoyant consciousness, without being aware of the fact. Once again it is necessary for the soul to be strengthened, in order that one may hold one's own, not only

78

as regards a spiritual outer world with which one blends, but
even as regards a spiritual entity which in a higher sense is one's
own self, and which nevertheless stands outside that which is
necessarily felt to be the self in the physical world. The way in
which the second self rises out of the waves of the soul's life, in
the form of a picture, yet essentially real, is quite different in
different human individualities. I have tried in the following
plays picturing the soul's life, "The Portal of Initiation," "The
Soul's Probation," "The Guardian of the Threshold," and "The
Awakening of the Soul," to portray how various human
individualities work their way through to the experience of this
"other self."

Now even if the soul in ordinary consciousness knows
nothing about its being inspired by its other self, yet that
inspiration is nevertheless there, in the depths of the soul. It is,
however, not expressed in thoughts or inner words; but takes
effect through deeds, through events or through something that
happens. It is the other self that guides the soul to the details of
its life's destiny, and calls forth capacities, inclinations,
aptitudes, and so forth within it. This other self lives in the sum-
total or aggregate of the destiny of a human life. It moves
alongside of the self which is conditioned by birth and death,
and shapes human life, with all that it contains of joy and
sorrow. When clairvoyant consciousness joins that other self, it
learns to say "I" to the total aggregate of the life-destiny, just as
physical man says "I" to his individual being. That which is
called by an Eastern word Karma, grows together in the way
that has been indicated, with the other self, or the spiritual ego.
The life of a human being is seen to be inspired by his own
permanent entity, which lives on from one life to another; and
the inspiration operates in such a way that the life-destiny of one
earthly existence is the direct consequence of previous ones.

Thus man learns to know himself as another being, different
from his physical personality, which indeed only comes to
expression in physical existence through the working of this
being. When the consciousness enters the world of that other
being, it is in a region which, as compared with the elemental
world, may be called the world of the spirit.

As long as we feel ourselves to be in that world, we find ourselves completely outside the sphere in which all the experiences and events of the physical world are enacted. We look from another world back upon the one which we have in a certain sense left behind. But we also arrive at the knowledge that, as human beings, we belong to both worlds. We feel the physical world to be a kind of reflected image of the world of the spirit. Yet this image, although reflecting the events and beings of the spiritual world, does not merely do this, but also leads an independent life of its own, although it is only an image. It is as though a person were to look into a mirror, and as though his reflected image were to come to independent life whilst he was looking at it.

Moreover, we learn to know spiritual beings who bring about this independent life of the reflected image of the spiritual world. We feel them to be beings who belong to the world of the spirit with regard to their origin, but who have left the arena of that world, and sought their field of action in the physical world. We thus find ourselves confronting two worlds which act one upon the other. We will call the spiritual world the higher, and the physical world the lower.

We learn to know these spiritual beings in the lower world through having to a certain extent transferred our point of view to the higher world. One class of these spiritual beings presents itself in such a way that through them we discover the reason why man experiences the physical world as substantial and material. We discover that everything material is in reality spiritual, and that the spiritual activity of these beings consolidates and hardens the spiritual element of the physical world into matter. However unpopular certain names are in the present day, they are needed for that which is seen as reality in the world of spirit. And so we will call the beings who bring about materialisation the Ahrimanic beings. It appears that their original sphere is the mineral kingdom. In that kingdom they reign in such a way that there they can bring fully into manifestation what is their real nature. In the vegetable kingdom and in the higher kingdoms of nature they accomplish something else, which only becomes intelligible when the

80

sphere of the elemental world is taken into account. Seen from the world of the spirit, the elemental world also appears like a reflection of that world. But the reflected image in the elemental world has not so much independence as that in the physical world. In the former, the spiritual beings of the Ahrimanic class are less dominant than in the latter. From the elemental world, however, they do develop, amongst other things, the kind of activity which comes to expression in annihilation and death. We may even say that in the higher kingdoms of nature the part of the Ahrimanic beings is to introduce death. So far as death is part of the necessary order of existence, the mission of the Ahrimanic beings is legitimate.

But when we view the activity of the Ahrimanic beings from the world of the spirit, we find that something else is connected with their work in the lower world. Inasmuch as their sphere of action is there, they do not feel bound to respect the limits which would restrain their activity if they were operating in the higher world from which they originate. In the lower world they struggle for an independence which they could never have in the higher sphere. This is especially evident in the influence of the Ahrimanic beings on man, inasmuch as man forms the highest kingdom of nature in the physical world. As far as the human life of the soul is bound up with physical existence, they strive to give that life independence, to wrench it free from the higher world, and to incorporate it entirely in the lower. Man as a thinking soul originates from the higher world. The thinking soul which has become clairvoyant also enters that higher world. But the thinking which is evolved in, and bound up with, the physical world, has in it that which must be called the influence of the Ahrimanic beings. These beings desire to give, as it were, a kind of permanent existence to a sense-bound thinking within the physical world. At the same time as their forces bring death, they desire to hold back the thinking soul from death, and only to allow the other principles of man to be carried away by the stream of annihilation. Their intention is that the human power of thought shall remain behind in the physical world and adopt a kind of existence approximating ever more and more to the Ahrimanic nature.

81

In the lower world what has just been described is only expressed through its effects. Man may strive to saturate himself in his thinking soul with the forces which recognise the spiritual world, and know themselves to live and have their being within it. But he may also turn away with his thinking soul from those forces, and only make use of his thought for laying hold of the physical world. Temptations to the latter course of action come from the Ahrimanic powers.

VI

Concerning the Astral Body and the Luciferic Beings; and the Nature of the Etheric Body

THERE is another group of spiritual beings, who from the world of the spirit are seen to be active in the physical world (and also in the elemental world), as in an adopted field of action. These are the spirits who desire to liberate the feeling soul entirely from the physical world, and therefore in a certain way to spiritualise it. Life in the physical world is part of the cosmic order of things. While the human soul is living in the physical world, it is passing through a development which is part of the conditions of its existence. Its being woven into the physical world is a result of the activity of beings whom one learns to know in the higher world. That activity is opposed by the beings who desire to wrench the feeling soul free from physical conditions. These latter beings may be called the Luciferic beings.

The Luciferic beings stand in the physical world searching as it were, for everything of a psychic nature (feeling) which is to be found there, in order that they may draw it out of the physical world and incorporate it in a cosmic sphere of their own, adapted to their nature. Seen from the higher world, the activity of these Luciferic beings is also ab-servable in the elemental world. Within this they strive to obtain a certain sphere of power which they want to disconnect from the grossness of the physical world, although that sphere has been preordained, by

83

the beings of the higher world, to be connected with the lower world. Just as the Ahrimanic beings would be keeping to their own sphere if they were only to bring about the temporary annihilation of existence which is based on the order of the cosmos, so the Luciferic beings would not be crossing the boundary of their own kingdom if they imbued the feeling soul with powers which would continually stimulate it to rise above the urgent necessities of the physical world, and feel itself, with regard to those necessities, a free and independent being. But the Luciferic beings go beyond the limits of their domain when they desire, in the face of the universal order of the higher world, to create a special spiritual kingdom for which they wish to remould the psychic beings in the physical world.

We can see how the influence of Luciferic beings in the physical world expands in two directions. On the one hand it is owing to them that man is able to rise above the bare experience of what is physically real. He is able to derive his joy, his uplifting, not only from the physical world; but can also take pleasure in and feel elated by that which exists merely in semblance, that which, as beauty transcends the physical. From this point of view the Luciferic beings have co-operated in bringing about the most important, and especially the artistic, features of civilisation. Moreover, man is able to enjoy unfettered thought; he need not merely describe physical things and portray them slavishly in his thoughts. He is able to develop creative thought beyond the physical world, and to philosophise about things. On the other hand, the exaggeration of the Luciferic forces in the soul is the source of much extravagance and confusion, for they try to develop the activities of the soul without adhering to the conditions of the higher cosmic order. Philosophising which is not based upon a thorough adherence to the cosmic order, headstrong indulgence in arbitrary ideas, excessive forcing of one's own personal predilections: all these things are the dark side of the Luciferic activity.

The human soul belongs, through its other self, to the higher world. But it also belongs to existence in the lower world. Clairvoyant consciousness, if it has passed through adequate preparation, feels itself as a conscious being in the higher world.

The facts of the case are not altered, but, to those facts which hold good for every human soul, there is added in clairvoyant consciousness, the knowledge of the facts. Every human soul belongs to the higher world, and when man is living in the physical world, he is associated with a physical body which is subject to the processes of the physical world. The soul is also associated with a subtle, etheric body, which lives subject to the processes of the elemental world. The Ahrimanic and Luciferic forces which are spiritual and supersensible work in both these bodies.

In so far as the human soul lives in the higher or spiritual world, it is what may be called an astral being. One of the many reasons which justify this expression is that the astral being of man as such is not subject to the conditions which prevail within the sphere of earth. Spiritual science recognises that within man's astral being are working, not the "natural" laws of earth, but those laws which have to be taken into account in considering the processes of the world of the stars (astra). On this account the term may appear justified. Thus the recognition of a third or astral body is added to that of the physical body and the subtle, etheric body of man. But it is necessary that the following should be borne in mind. As regards its original essence, man's astral body has its origin in the higher world, in the spiritual world proper. Within that sphere it is a being of the same nature as other beings whose activity is exercised in that world. Inasmuch then as the elemental and physical worlds are reflections of the spiritual world, the etheric and physical bodies of man must also be looked upon as reflections of his astral being. But in those bodies forces are working, which originate from the Luciferic and Ahrimanic beings. Now since those beings have a spiritual origin, it is natural that within the region of the etheric and physical bodies themselves there thould be found a kind of human astral essence. And a degree of clairvoyance which merely accepts the pictures of clairvoyant consciousness, without being able rightly to understand their meaning, may easily take the astral admixture in the physical and etheric bodies for the astral body proper. Yet that human astral essence is just that principle of human nature which

opposes man's conforming to the laws really suitable for him in
the order of the cosmos. Mistakes and confusions are more
easily made in this domain because a knowledge of the soul's
astral being is at the outset quite impossible for ordinary human
consciousness. Even during the first stages of clairvoyant
consciousness such knowledge is not yet attainable. The
consciousness is attained when man experiences himself in his
etheric body. But in this body he beholds the reflected images of
his other self, and the higher world to which he belongs. In this
way also he beholds the reflected etheric image of his astral
body, and at the same time the Luciferic and Ahrimanic beings
which that body contains.

It will be shewn later in this work that the ego too, which man
in ordinary life looks upon as his entity, is not the real ego, but
only the reflection of the real ego in the physical world. In the
same way the etheric reflection of the astral body may, in etheric
clairvoyance, become an illusory image mistaken for the real
astral body.

When one penetrates further into the higher world,
clairvoyant consciousness also succeeds in gaining a true insight
as regards human beings into the nature of the reflection of the
higher world in the lower. It then becomes supremely evident
that the subtle, etheric body, which man bears about him in his
present earthly existence, is not really the reflected image of that
which corresponds to this body in the higher world. It is a
reflected image altered by the activity of the Lucerific and
Ahrimanic beings. The spiritual archetype of the etheric body is
not able to reflect itself at all perfectly in man on earth, owing to
the nature of the earthly essence in which the beings mentioned
above are active. If clairvoyant consciousness betakes itself
beyond the earth to a region in which a perfect reflection of the
archetype of the etheric body is possible, it finds itself carried
back to a remote past, previous to the present condition of the
earth, before even the "Moon condition" which preceded it. It
arrives at an insight into the manner in which the present earth
was evolved out of a "Moon condition," and the latter again out
of a "Sun condition." Further particulars as to why the terms
"Sun" and "Moon" condition are justified will be found in my

86

Occult Science.

The earth, then, was once in a Sun condition, out of which it evolved to a Moon condition, and afterwards became earth. During the Sun condition the etheric body of man was an absolute reflection of the spiritual events and beings of the world from which it originates. Clairvoyant consciousness discovers that those Sun beings were made up of pure wisdom. Thus we may say that, during the earth's Sun condition in a remote past, man received his etheric body as a pure reflection of cosmic beings of Wisdom. Later, during the Moon and Earth conditions, the etheric body has become changed into that which it now is as a part of the human being.

VII

Summary of the Foregoing

MAN bears within him a soul-centre belonging to a spiritual world. This is the permanent human entity, which passes through repeated earthly lives in such a way that in one earthly life it is trained in normal consciousness as a being independent of that consciousness, then experiences itself in a purely spiritual world, after human physical death, and in due time realises in a new earthly life the results of the preceding one. This permanent entity acts as the inspirer of man's destiny in such a way that one earthly life follows another as a consequence which is based on the order of the cosmos.

Man is this permanent entity itself; he lives in it as though in his other self. Inasmuch as he, as a being, is that other self, so he lives in an astral body, in the same way as he is living in a physical and etheric body. Just as the environment of the physical body is the physical world and that of the etheric body the elemental world, so the environment of the astral body is the world of the spirit.

Beings of the same nature and origin as man's other self are working in the physical and elemental worlds as Ahrimanic and Luciferic powers. The way in which they work makes the relation of the astral body to the etheric and physical bodies intelligible.

The original source of the etheric body is to be found in a long-past period of the earth, its so-called Sun condition.

88

In accordance with the foregoing, the following survey of man may be made:—

I. The physical body in the environment of the physical world. By means of this body man recognises himself as an independent individual (ego).

II. The subtle (etheric or vital) body in the elemental environment. By means of this body man recognises himself as a member of the earth's vital body, and hence indirectly as a member of three successive planetary states.

III. The astral body in a purely spiritual environment. Through this body man is a member of a spiritual world of which the elemental and physical worlds are reflections. In the astral body lives man's other self, and this comes to expression in repeated earthly lives.

VIII

Concerning the Guardian of the Threshold and some Peculiarities of Clairvoyant Consciousness

AS far as his experiences in the physical world are concerned, man is outside the spiritual world, in which, as has been stated in the preceding pages, his real being is rooted. The part played by physical experience in human nature is realised when we consider that for clairvoyant consciousness, which enters the supersensitive worlds, it is necessary to strengthen those very forces of the soul which are acquired in the physical world. If this strengthening has not taken place, the soul feels a certain timidity in entering the supersensible world. It even tries to avoid an entrance by seeking proofs of its impossibility.

But if the soul finds that it is strong enough to enter, if it recognises in itself the forces which allow it, after entering, to maintain itself there as an independent being, and to experience in its field of consciousness not only thoughts but beings, as must be the case in the elemental and spiritual worlds, then the soul also feels that only by life in the physical world has it been enabled to gather those forces. It realises the necessity of being led through the physical world on its journey through the universe.

The realisation of this especially results from the experience in thoughts through which clairvoyant consciousness passes. On entering the elemental world, the consciousness becomes filled with beings who are perceived in the form of pictures. In that world it is not able to develop with regard to these beings an inner activity of the soul similar to that which is developed in thought-life within the physical world. Yet it would be impossible to find one's way as a human being within the elemental world if we did not enter it as thinking beings. We might certainly behold the beings of the elemental world without thinking about them, but we should not know what any of them really were. We should be like a man looking at writing which he cannot read; he sees with his eyes exactly the same thing as is seen by one who can read it, but it only has meaning and substance for the latter.

Nevertheless clairvoyant consciousness during its sojourn in the elemental world exercises by no means the same kind of thought-activity as is carried on in the physical world. Rather is it the case that a thinking being—such as man—in the act of beholding the elemental world also perceives the meaning of its beings and forces, while a non-thinking being would see the pictures without understanding their meaning and essence.

On entering the spiritual world, the Ahrimanic beings, for instance, would be taken for something quite different from what they really are if they were beheld by the soul of a non-thinking being. It is the same with the Luciferic and other beings of the spiritual world. The Ahrimanic and Luciferic beings are only beheld by man in their true reality if he contemplates them from the spiritual world with clairvoyant sight which has been strengthened by thinking.

If the soul did not arm itself with adequate power for thought, the Luciferic beings, when seen from the spiritual world, would take possession of the world of clairvoyant pictures and bring about in the contemplating soul the illusion that it was penetrating ever more deeply into the spiritual world which it was really seeking, whereas actually it would be sinking deeper and deeper into the world which the Luciferic forces desire to prepare similar to their own being. The soul would certainly feel itself becoming more independent, but it would be adapting itself to a spiritual world not in keeping with its own nature and origin. It would be entering a spiritual environment foreign to it.

The physical world conceals from view such beings as the

Luciferic ones. Therefore, within that world they are not able to mislead the consciousness. They are simply non-existent as far as this consciousness is concerned, and, not being misled by them, it is able to strengthen itself adequately by thought. It is one of the instinctive peculiarities of healthy consciousness that it only desires to enter the spiritual world in proportion as it has sufficiently strengthened itself in the physical world for beholding the spiritual world. Consciousness clings to the way in which it experiences itself in the physical world. It feels itself to be in its own element when it can experience itself by means of the thoughts, feelings, emotions, etc., which it owes to the physical world. The tenacity with which consciousness clings to this kind of experience is especially apparent at the actual moment of entering supersensible worlds. Just as a person at particular moments of his life clings to dear memories, so at the entrance to supersensible worlds do there of necessity ascend from the depths of the soul all possible affections of which the individual is capable. We then become aware how strongly we cleave to that life which connects man with the physical world. This attachment to earth-life then appears in its full reality, stripped of our usual illusions. At the entrance to the supersensible world, and, as it were, at the first supersensible achievement—a certain self-knowledge is brought about, of which we can previously have had scarcely any idea. And we see how much we have to leave behind if we really desire to enter knowingly into that world in which, after all, we are always actually present. What we have made of ourselves as human beings, consciously and unconsciously in the physical world comes before the soul with the most vivid distinctness.

The result of this experience is often that all further attempts at penetrating into supersensible worlds are abandoned. For we then clearly realise the necessity of changing our way of thinking and feeling, if our sojourn in the spiritual world is to be successful. We have to make up our minds to develop quite a different attitude of soul from the one that has hitherto been ours, or, in other words, a different attitude must be added to the one we have already acquired.

And yet—what is it that really happens at the moment of

entering the supersensible world? We see the being which we
have always been; but we do not now see it from the physical
world, from which we have always seen it hitherto; we see it,
free from illusions, in its true reality, from the standpoint of the
spiritual world. We behold it in such a way that we feel
ourselves permeated with those powers of cognition which are
able to measure it according to its spiritual worth. When we see
ourselves thus, it becomes plain why we hesitate about
consciously entering the supersensible world; the degree of
strength becomes apparent, which it is necessary to have before
entering it. We see how, even with knowledge, we keep at a
distance from that world. And the more accurately we thus see
through ourselves, the more strongly do those affections come to
the front by means of which we desire to continue to keep our
consciousness in the physical world. Our increased knowledge
entices those affections out of their lurking-places in the depths
of the soul. We must, however, recognise them, for only by so
doing are they overcome. But even when recognised they still
manifest their power in quite a remarkable way. They desire to
subdue the soul, which feels itself drawn down by them as if
into unknown depths. The moment of self-recognition is a
serious one. Far too much philosophising and theorising about
self-knowledge goes on in the world. The soul's gaze is thereby
rather turned away from, than drawn towards, the earnestness
connected with real self-knowledge. And yet, in spite of this
necessary earnestness, it affords a great satisfaction to know that
human nature is so ordered that its instincts prevent it from
entering the spiritual world before it is able to develop within
itself, as self-experience, the necessary state of maturity. What a
satisfaction it is that the first momentous meeting with a being
of the supersensible world is the meeting with our own being in
its true reality which will guide us further in human evolution.

We may say that there is hidden within man a being that
keeps careful watch and ward on the boundary which has to be
crossed at the entrance to the supersensible world. This spiritual
being, hidden in man, which is man himself, but which he can as
little perceive with ordinary consciousness as the eye can see
itself, is the guardian of the threshold of the spiritual world. We

learn to recognise him at the moment at which we are not only actually he, but are also confronting him, as though we were standing outside him, and he were another being.

As with other experiences of supersensible worlds, it is the strengthened and reinforced faculties of the soul which make visible the guardian of the threshold. For, setting aside the fact that the meeting with the guardian becomes raised into knowledge by clairvoyant spiritual sight, that meeting is not an event which happens only to the man who has become clairvoyant. Exactly the same fact as is represented by this meeting happens to every human being every time he falls asleep, and we are confronting ourselves—which is the same thing as standing before the guardian of the threshold—for so long as our sleep lasts. During sleep the soul rises to its supersensible nature. But its inner forces are not then strong enough to bring about consciousness of itself.

In order to understand clairvoyant experience, especially in its early beginnings, it is particularly important to bear in mind that the soul may already have begun to live in the supersensible world before it is able to formulate to itself any knowledge worthy of the name. Clairvoyance at first appears in a very subtle way, so that often, inasmuch, as they expect to see something almost tangible, people do not need clairvoyant impressions which are flitting by, and will in no way recognise them as such. In this case the impressions sink into oblivion almost as soon as they appear. They enter the field of consciousness so slightly that they remain quite unnoticed, like tiny clouds on the soul's horizon.

On this account, and because people for the most part expect clairvoyance to be quite different from what it at first is, it often remains undiscovered by many earnest seekers after the spiritual world. In this respect too the meeting with the guardian of the threshold is important. If the soul has been strengthened just in the direction of self-knowledge, this very meeting may merely be like the first gentle flitting-by of a spiritual vision; but it will not be so easily consigned to oblivion as other supersensible impressions, because people are more interested in their own being than in other things.

There is, however, no need at all that the meeting with the guardian should be one of the first clairvoyant experiences. The soul may be strengthened in various directions, and the first of such directions may bring other beings or events within its spiritual horizon before the meeting with the guardian takes place. Yet this meeting is sure to occur comparatively soon after entering the supersensible world.

IX

Concerning the Ego-Feeling
and the Human Soul's Capacity for Love;
and the Relation of these to the Elemental World

WHEN the human soul consciously enters the elemental world, it finds itself obliged to change many of the ideas which it acquired in the physical world; but if the soul strengthens its forces to a corresponding degree, it will be quite fit for the change. Only if it shrinks from the effort of this acquiring strength, may it be seized by the feeling of losing, on entering the elemental world, the firm basis on which it must build up its inner life. The ideas which are gained in the physical world only offer an impediment to entering the elemental world as long as we try to keep them in exactly the same form in which we gained them. There is, however, no reason except habit for adhering to them in this way. It is also quite natural that the consciousness, which at first only lives in the physical world, should be accustomed to look upon the form of its ideas which it has shaped there, as the only possible one. And it is even more than natural, it is necessary. The life of the soul would never attain its inner solidarity, its necessary stability, if it did not develop a consciousness in the physical world which in a certain respect lived in fixed ideas, rigorously forced upon it. Through everything which life in the physical world can give the soul, is it able to enter the elemental world in such a way that it does not lose its independence and firmness of nature there.

96

Strengthening and reinforcement of the life of the soul must be gained in order that that independence may not only be present as an unconscious quality of the soul on entering the elemental world, but may also be kept clearly in the consciousness. If the soul is too weak for conscious experience in the elemental world, on entering it the independence vanishes, just as a thought does which is not imprinted with sufficient clearness on the soul to live on as a distinct memory. In this case the soul cannot really enter the supersensible world at all with its consciousness. When it makes the attempt to enter, it is again and again thrown back into the physical world, by the being living within the soul which may be called the guardian of the threshold. And even if the soul has, so to speak, nibbled at the supersensible world, so that on sinking back into the physical world it retains something of the supersensible in its consciousness, such spoil from another sphere often only causes confusion in the life of thought. It is quite impossible to fall into such confusion if the faculty of sound judgment, as it may be acquired in the physical world, be adequately cultivated. By thus reinforcing the faculty of judgment, the soul will develop the right relation to the events and beings of supersensible worlds. For in order to live consciously in those worlds, an attitude of the soul is necessary which cannot be developed in the physical world with the same intensity with which it appears in supersensible worlds. This is the attitude of surrender to what is being experienced. We must steep ourselves in the experience and identify ourselves with it; and we must be able to do this to such a degree that we see ourselves outside our own being and feel ourselves within some other being. A transformation of our own being into the other with which we are having the experience must take place. If we do not possess this faculty of transformation, we cannot experience anything genuine in supersensible worlds. For there all experience is due to our being able to realise this feeling, "Now I am transformed in a certain definite way; now I am vitally present in a being which through its nature transforms mine in this particular way." This transformation of self, this conscious projection of oneself into other beings, is life in supersensible worlds. By this process of

97

conscious self-projection into others, we learn to know the beings and events of those worlds. We come to notice that with one being we have a certain degree of affinity; but that, by virtue of our own nature, we are further removed from another. Variations of inner experience come into view, which, especially in the elemental world, we must call sympathies and antipathies. For on encountering a being or event of the elemental world, we feel an experience emerging in the soul which may be denoted sympathy. By this experience we recognise the nature of the elemental being or event. But we must not think that experiences of sympathy and antipathy are only of account in proportion to their intensity or degree. In the physical world it is indeed in a certain sense true that we only speak of a strong or weak sympathy or antipathy as the case may be. In the elemental world, sympathies and antipathies are not only distinguishable by their intensity, but also in the same way as, for instance, colours may be distinguished from each other in the physical world. Just as we have a physical world of many colours, so can we experience an elemental world containing many sympathies or antipathies. It has also to be taken into account that antipathy in the elemental realm does not carry with it the meaning that we inwardly turn away from the thing so described; by antipathetic we simply mean a quality of the elemental being or event which bears a similar relation to the sympathetic quality of another event or being as does blue to red in the physical world.

We may speak of a "sense" which man is able to awaken for the elemental world in his etheric body. This sense is capable of perceiving sympathies and antipathies in the elemental world just as the eye becomes aware of colours and the ear of sounds in the physical world. And just as there one object is red and another blue, so the beings of the elemental world are such that one radiates a certain kind of sympathy, and another a certain kind of antipathy to our spiritual sight.

This experience of the elemental world through sympathies and antipathies is again something not confined to the clairvoyantly awakened soul; it is always at hand for every human soul, being part of its nature. But in the ordinary life of the soul the knowledge of this part of human nature is not developed. Man bears within him his etheric body; and through it is connected in manifold ways with beings and events of the elemental world. At one moment of his life he is woven with sympathies and antipathies into the elemental world in one way; at another moment in another way.

The soul, however, cannot continuously so live as an etheric being that sympathies and antipathies are always active and clearly expressed within it. Just as waking life alternates with sleep in physical existence, so does a different state contrast with that of experiencing sympathies and antipathies in the elemental world. The soul may withdraw from all sympathies and antipathies and experience itself alone, regarding and feeling merely its own being. Indeed, this feeling may reach such a degree of intensity that we may speak of willing our own being. It is then a question of a condition of the soul's life not easy to describe, because in its pure, original nature it is of such a kind that nothing in the physical world resembles it except the strong, unalloyed ego-feeling or feeling of self in the soul. As far as the elemental world is concerned we may describe this state as one in which the soul feels the impulse to say to itself with regard to the necessary surrender to experiences of sympathy and antipathy: "I will keep entirely to myself and within myself." And by a species of development of will the soul wrenches itself free from the state of surrender to the elemental experiences of sympathy and antipathy. This life in the self is, as it were, the sleeping state of the elemental world; whereas the surrender to events and beings is the waking state. When the human soul is awake in the elemental world and develops a wish to experience itself only, that is to say, feels the need of elemental sleep, it can obtain this by returning to the waking state of physical life with a fully developed feeling of self. For such experience, saturated with the feeling of self, in the physical world is synonymous with elemental sleep. It consists in the soul's being torn away from elemental experiences. It is literally true that to clairvoyant consciousness the life of the soul in the physical world is a spiritual sleep.

When awakening to the supersensible world takes place in

rightly developed human clairvoyance, the memory of the soul's experiences in the physical world still remains. It must remain, otherwise other beings and events would be present in clairvoyant consciousness, but not the clairvoyant's own being. We should in that case have no knowledge of ourselves; we should not be living in the spirit ourselves; but other beings and events would be living in our soul. Taking this into consideration, it will be clear that rightly developed clairvoyance must lay great stress on the cultivation of a strong ego-feeling. This ego-feeling developed with clairvoyance is by no means something which only enters the soul through clairvoyance; it is merely that we get to know that which always exists in the depths of the soul, but which remains unknown to the soul's ordinary life as it runs its course in the physical world.

The strong ego-feeling is not there through the etheric body as such, but through the soul which experiences itself in the physical body. If the soul does not bring that feeling with it into the clairvoyant state from its experience in the physical world, it will prove insufficiently equipped for experience in the elemental world.

On the other hand, it is essential for human consciousness within the physical world that the soul's feeling of self, its experience of the ego, although it must exist, should be modified. By this means it is possible for the soul to undergo within the physical world training for the noblest of moral forces, that of fellow-feeling, or feeling with another. If the strong ego-feeling were to project itself into the soul's conscious experiences within the physical world, moral impulses and ideas could not develop in the right way. They could not bring forth the fruit of love. But the faculty of self-surrender, a natural impulse in the elemental world, is not to be put on a par with what is called love in human experience. Elemental self-surrender means experiencing oneself in another being or event; love is the experiencing another being in one's own soul. In order to develop the latter experience, the feeling of self, or ego-experience, present in the depths of the soul, must have, as it were, a veil drawn over it; and in consequence of the soul's own forces being thus dulled, one is able to feel within oneself the

100

sorrows and joys of the other being: love, which is the source of all genuine morality in human life, springs up. Love is the most important result for man of his experience in the physical world. If we analyse the nature of love or fellow-feeling, we find it is the way in which spiritual reality is expressed in the physical world. It has already been said that it is in the nature of what is supersensible to become transformed into something else. If what is spiritual in man as he lives the physical life becomes so transformed that it dulls the ego-feeling and lives again as love, the spiritual remains true to its own elemental laws. We may say that on becoming clairvoyantly conscious the human soul awakes in the spiritual world; but we must say just as much that in love the spiritual awakens in the physical world. Where love and fellow-feeling are stirring in life, we sense the tragic breath of the spirit, interpenetrating the physical world. Hence rightly developed clairvoyance can never weaken sympathy or love. The more completely the soul becomes at home in spiritual worlds, the more it feels lovelessness and lack of fellow-feeling to be a denial of spirit itself.

The experiences of consciousness which is becoming clairvoyant, manifest special peculiarities with regard to what has just been stated. Whereas the ego-feeling—necessary as it is for experience in supersensible worlds—is easily deadened, and often behaves like a weak, fading thought in the memory, feelings of hatred and lovelessness, and immoral impulses become intense experiences immediately after entering the supersensible world. They appear before the soul like reproaches come to life, and become terribly real pictures. In order not to be tormented by them, clairvoyant consciousness often has recourse to the expedient of looking about for spiritual forces which weaken the impressions of these pictures. But by doing so the soul steeps itself in these forces, which have an injurious effect on the newly-won clairvoyance. They drive it out of the good regions of the spiritual world, and towards the bad ones.

On the other hand, true love and real kindness of heart are experiences of the soul which strengthen the forces of consciousness in the way necessary for acquiring clairvoyance.

When it is said that the soul needs preparation before it is able to have experiences in the supersensible world, it should be added that one of the many means of preparation is the capacity for true love, and the disposition towards genuine human kindness and fellow-feeling.

An over-developed ego-feeling in the physical world works against morality. An ego-feeling too feebly developed causes the soul, around which the storms of elemental sympathies and antipathies are actually playing to be lacking in inner firmness and stability. These qualities can only exist when a sufficiently strong ego-feeling is working out of the experiences of the physical world upon the etheric body, which of course remains unknown in ordinary life. But in order to develop a really moral temper of mind it is necessary that the ego-feeling, though it must exist, should be moderated by feelings of good-fellowship, sympathy, and love.

X

Concerning the Boundary between the Physical World and Supersensible Worlds

IN order to understand the mutual relations of the various worlds, we must take into account the fact that a force which in one world is bound to develop activity in conformity with the order of the universe, may, when it comes to be developed in another world, be directed against that order. Therefore it is necessary for man's being that there should exist in his etheric body the two opposing forces, the capacity for transformation into other beings, and the strong ego-feeling, or feeling of self. Neither of these forces of the human soul can be unfolded in physical existence except in a deadened form. In the elemental world they exist in such a way as to make man's being possible by their mutual balance, just as sleep and the waking state make human life in the physical world possible. The relation of two such opposing forces can never be that of one effacing the other, but must be of such a kind that both are developed and act upon each other in the way of balance or compensation.

Now it is only in the elemental world that the ego-feeling and the capacity for transformation act upon each other in the way indicated; the physical world can only be worked upon, in conformity with the order of the universe, by the result of these two forces in their mutual relationship and co-operation. If the capacity for transformation which it is necessary for a person to possess in his etheric body were to extend in the same degree to

103

physical existence, he would feel himself in his soul as something which in considering his physical body he is not. The physical body gives man in its own world a certain fixed stamp, by means of which he is put into that world as a particular personal being. He is not put into the elemental world with his etheric body in this manner. In the elemental world, in order to be a human being in the full sense, he must be able to assume the most varied forms. If this were impossible to him, he would be condemned to complete isolation in the elemental world; he would not be able to know about anything in it except himself; for he would not feel himself related to any other being or event. This, in the elemental world would be equivalent to the non-existence of those beings or events, as far as such a person was concerned.

If, however, the human soul were to develop in the physical world the capacity for transformation necessary for the elemental world, its personal identity would be lost. Such a soul would be living in contradiction with itself. In the physical world, the capacity for transformation must be a power at rest in the depths of the soul; a power which gives the soul its fundamental tone or keynote, but which does not come to development in that world.

Clairvoyant consciousness has therefore to live itself into the capacity for transformation; if it were not able to do this, it could make no observations in the elemental world. It thus acquires a faculty which it should only bring to bear so long as it knows itself to be in the elemental world, and which it must suppress as soon as it returns to the physical world. Clairvoyant consciousness must ever observe the boundary of the two worlds, and must not use in the physical world faculties adapted for a supersensible world. If the soul, knowing itself to be in the physical world, were to allow the capacity for transformation possessed by its etheric body to go on working, ordinary consciousness would become filled with conceptions which do not correspond to any being in the physical world. Confusion would reign in the life of the soul's thought. Observation of the boundary between the worlds is a necessary presupposition for the right working of clairvoyant consciousness. One who wants to acquire this consciousness must be careful that no disturbing element creeps into his ordinary consciousness through his knowledge of supersensible worlds.

If we learn to know the guardian of the threshold we know the state of our soul with regard to the physical world, and whether it is strong enough to banish from physical consciousness the forces and faculties, belonging to supersensible worlds, which should not be allowed to be active in ordinary consciousness. If the supersensible world is entered without the self-knowledge brought about by the guardian of the threshold, we may be overwhelmed by the experiences of that world. These experiences may thrust themselves into physical consciousness as illusive pictures. In that case they assume the character of sense-perceptions, and the necessary consequence is that the soul takes them for realities when they are not so. Rightly developed clairvoyance will never take the pictures of the elemental world for reality in the sense in which physical consciousness has to take the experiences of the physical world as realities. The pictures of the elemental world are only brought into their true association with the realities to which they correspond, by the soul's faculty of transformation.

Again, the second force necessary for the etheric body—the strong ego-feeling—should not be projected into the soul's life within the physical world in the same way as is appropriate for it in the elemental world. If it is, it then becomes a source of immoral propensities, as far as these are connected with egoism. It is at this point in its observation of the universe that spiritual science finds the origin of evil in human action. It would be misunderstanding the order of the world to surrender oneself to the belief that this order could be maintained without the forces which form the source of evil. If these forces were non-existent, the etheric being of man could not come to development in the elemental world. These forces are entirely good when they come into operation in the elemental world only. They bring about evil when they do not remain at rest in the depths of the soul, there regulating man's relation to the elemental world, but are transferred to the soul's experience within the physical world and are changed thereby into selfish impulses. In this case they work against the faculty of love and thus become the causes of immoral action.

If the strong ego-feeling passes from the etheric to the physical body, it not only effects a strengthening of egoism, but a weakening of the etheric body. Clairvoyant consciousness has to make the discovery that on entering the supersensible world, the necessary ego-feeling is weak in proportion as egoism in the experiences of the physical world is strong. Egoism does not make a human being strong in the depths of his soul, but weak. And when man passes through the gateway of death, the effect of the egoism which has been developed during the life between birth and death is such as to make the soul weak for the experiences of the supersensible world.

XI

Concerning Beings of the Spirit-Worlds

IF the soul enters the supersensible world with clairvoyant consciousness, it learns to know itself there in a way of which in the physical world it can have no conception. It finds that through its faculty of transformation it becomes acquainted with beings to whom it is more or less related; but in addition to this it becomes aware of meeting beings in the supersensible world to whom it is not only related, but with whom it must compare itself, in order to know itself. And it further observes that these beings in supersensible worlds have become what the soul itself, through its adventures and experiences in the physical world, has become. In the elemental world beings confront the human soul who have developed within that world powers and faculties which man himself can only unfold through still having about him his physical body, in addition to his etheric body and the other supersensible principles of his being. The beings here alluded to have no such body with physical senses. They have so evolved that through their etheric body they have a soul-nature such as man has through his physical body. Although to a certain degree they are beings of like nature to himself, they differ from him in not being subject to the conditions of the physical world. They have no senses of the kind which man possesses. Their knowledge is like man's; only they have not acquired it through the gateway of the senses, but through a kind of ascent, or mounting-up of their ideas and other soul-

107

experiences out of the depths of their being. Their inner life is, as it were, at rest within them, and they draw it up out of the depths of their souls, as man from the depths of his soul draws up his memory-pictures.

In this way man becomes acquainted with beings who have become within the supersensible world that which he may become within the physical world. Owing to this, these beings are a stage higher than man in the order of the universe, although they may be said to be, in the manner indicated, of the same nature as he. They constitute a kingdom above man, a hierarchy superior to him in the scale of beings. Notwithstanding their similarity to man, their etheric body is different from his. Whereas man is woven into the supersensible etheric body of the earth through the sympathies and antipathies of his etheric body, these beings are not earth-bound in the life of their soul.

If man observes what these beings experience through their etheric bodies, he finds that their experiences are similar to those of his own soul. They have thinking power; they have feelings and a will. But through their etheric body they develop something which man can only develop through the physical body. Through their etheric body they arrive at a consciousness of their own being, although man would not be able to know anything about a supersensible being unless he carried up into supersensible worlds the forces which he acquires in the physical body.

Clairvoyant consciousness learns to know these beings through developing a faculty for observing them by the help of the human etheric body. This clairvoyant consciousness lifts the human soul up into the world in which these beings have their field of activity and their abode. Not till the soul experiences itself in that world, do pictures or conceptions arise in its consciousness which bring about knowledge of these beings. For these beings do not interpose directly in the physical world, nor therefore in man's physical body. They are not present in the experiences which may be made through that body. They are spiritual, supersensible beings, who do not, so to say, set toot in the physical world.

If man does not respect the boundary between the physical world and supersensible worlds, it may happen that he drags into his physical consciousness supersensible images which are not the true expression of these beings. These images arise through experiencing the Luciferic and Ahrimanic beings, who though of like nature to the supersensible beings just described, are contrasted with them through having transferred their field of activity and their abodes to the world which man perceives as the physical world.

When man with clairvoyant consciousness contemplates the Luciferic and Ahrimanic beings from the supersensible world, after having through his experience with the guardian of the threshold, learned the right way to observe the boundary between that world and physical existence, he learns to know these beings in their reality, and to distinguish them from those other spiritual beings who have remained in the sphere of action adapted to their nature. It is from this standpoint that spiritual science must portray the Luciferic and Ahrimanic beings.

It then appears that the field of activity adapted to the Luciferic beings is not the physical but, in a certain respect, the elemental world. When something penetrates into the human soul which rises as though out of the waves of that world like pictures, and when these pictures work with a vivifying effect on man's etheric body, without assuming an illusive existence in the soul, then the Luciferic essence may be present in these images, without its activity transgressing against the order of the universe. In this case the Luciferic nature has the effect of emancipation upon the human soul, raising it above mere entanglement in the physical world. But when the human soul draws into the physical body the life which it should only develop in the elemental world, when it allows feeling within the physical body to be influenced by sympathies and antipathies which should only hold sway in the etheric body, then the Luciferic nature gains through that soul an influence which is opposed to the general order of the universe. This influence is always present when in the sympathies and antipathies of the physical world, something is working besides that love which is based on sympathy with the life of another being present in that world. Such a being may be loved because it comes before the one loving it endowed with certain qualities; in this case there is no admixture of a Luciferic element with the love. Love which has its basis in those qualities in the beloved being which are manifest in physical existence, keeps clear of Luciferic interference. But love, the source of which is not thus in the beloved being, but in the one loving it, is prone to the Luciferic influence. A being loved because it has qualities to which, as lovers, we incline by nature, is loved with that part of the soul which is accessible to the Luciferic element.

We should therefore never say that the Luciferic element is bad under all circumstances, for events and beings of supersensible worlds must be loved by the human soul in the manner of the Luciferic element. The order of the universe is not transgressed until the kind of love with which man ought to feel himself drawn to the supersensible is directed to physical things. Love for the supersensible rightly calls forth in the one loving it an enhanced feeling of self; love which in the physical world is sought for the sake of such an enhanced feeling of self is equivalent to a Luciferic temptation. Love of the spiritual when it is sought for the sake of the self has the effect of emancipation; but love for the physical when it is sought on account of the self has not this effect, but, through the gratification gained by its means, only puts the self in fetters.

The Ahrimanic beings make themselves felt in the thinking soul just as the Luciferic beings affect the feeling soul. The former chain thought to the physical world. They turn it away from the fact that thoughts of any kind are only of importance when they assert themselves as part of the universal order, whose discovery is not bound within physical existence. In the world into which the human life of the soul is woven, the Ahrimanic element must exist as a necessary counterbalance to the Luciferic. Without the Luciferic element, the soul would dream away its life in observation of physical existence, and feel no impulse to rise above it. Without the counter-effect of the Ahrimanic element, the soul would fall a victim to the Luciferic influence; it would underrate the importance of the physical world, in spite of the fact that some of its necessary conditions of existence are in that world. It would not wish to have anything to do with the physical world. The Ahrimanic element has the right degree of importance in the human soul when it leads to a way of living in the physical world which is suitable to that world; when we take it for what it is, and are able to dispense with everything in it which in its nature must be transitory.

It is quite impossible to say that a person could avoid falling a victim to the Luciferic and Ahrimanic elements by rooting them out of himself. It is, for instance, possible that if the Luciferic element in him were rooted out, his soul would no longer aspire to the supersensible; or, if the Ahrimanic element were eradicated, that he might not any more realise the full importance of the physical world: the right relation to one of these elements is arrived at when the proper counterpoise to it is provided in the other. All harmful effects from these cosmic beings proceed entirely from one of them becoming the unlimited master of the situation, whatever it may be, and from not being brought into the right harmony through the opposite force.

XII

Concerning Spiritual Cosmic Beings

WHEN clairvoyant consciousness comes to life in the elemental world, it finds beings there who are able to develop a life in that world which man only acquires within the physical world. These beings do not feel their self—their ego—as man feels his in the physical world; they permeate that self with their will much more than man does his; they will their own existence as it were, and feel their existence as something which they give to themselves through their will. On the other hand, with regard to their thinking, they have not the feeling that they are creating their thoughts, as man creates his; they feel all their thoughts as suggestions, as something which is not in them but in the universe, and which is streaming out of the universe into their being. Thus in these beings no doubt can ever arise but that their thoughts are the reflection of the thought-order poured forth into the universe. They do not think their own thoughts, but cosmic thoughts. With their activity of thought they live in cosmic thoughts; but they will their existence. Their life of feeling is shaped in accordance with this will and thought of theirs. They feel themselves to be a link in the whole cosmic system; and they feel the necessity of willing their existence in a manner corresponding to that system.

When the clairvoyant soul grows familiar with the world inhabited by these beings, it comes naturally to an idea of its own thinking, feeling, and willing. These faculties of the human soul could not be unfolded within the elemental world in man's etheric body. Human will would be only a weak, dreamlike faculty in the elemental world, human thought merely an indistinct, fleeting world of ideas. No feeling of the ego would come into existence there at all. For all these things it is necessary for man to be invested with a physical body.

When the clairvoyant human soul ascends from the elemental world into the spiritual world proper, it experiences itself in conditions which diverge still further than do elemental conditions from those of the physical world. In the elemental world there is still much that is reminiscent of the physical world; but in the spiritual world man confronts entirely new conditions. He can do nothing there if he has only the ideas which are to be gained in the physical world. All the same, man's inner life as a human soul in the physical world must be so strengthened that he will bring over from that world into the spiritual world that which makes a sojourn there possible. If such a strengthened life of the soul were not brought into the spiritual world, man would simply lapse into unconsciousness there. He could only be present there in the same sort of way in which a plant is present in the physical world. We have, as human souls, to bring with us into the spiritual world all those things not really existing in the physical world but manifesting themselves there nevertheless as if they were existent. We must be able to form conceptions in the physical world, which, though prompted by that world, do not directly correspond to any thing or occurrence in it. Every delineation of things in the physical world, or description of physical occurrences, is meaningless in the spiritual world. What may be perceived with the senses, or expressed in conceptions applicable in the physical world, does not exist in the spiritual world. On entering the latter, everything to which physical ideas can be applied must, so to speak, be left behind. But ideas which have been so formed in the physical world that they do not correspond to any physical thing or process, are still present in the soul when it enters the spiritual world. Naturally some of these ideas may have been formed erroneously. If these are present in the consciousness on its entering the spiritual world, by their very being they prove themselves as not belonging to that world. They act in such a way as to impress on the soul the urgency of returning to the physical world or the elemental world, in order to exchange these erroneous ideas for the right ones. But when the soul brings correct ideas into the spiritual world, what is related to them in that world presses to meet them; the soul feels in the spiritual world that actual beings are present there, who actually are in their whole inner substance what only appear as thoughts within itself. These beings have a body, which may be called a thought-body. In this body they experience themselves as independent beings, just as man experiences himself independently with the physical world.

Now amongst the conceptions acquired by man, there are certain thoughts saturated with feelings which are adapted to strengthen the life of the soul in such a way that it is able to receive an impression from the beings of the spiritual world. When the feeling of self-surrender, such as must be developed for the faculty of transformation in the elemental world, becomes so much intensified that in that surrender the being into which we are transformed is felt not merely as sympathetic or antipathetic, but can live again in its own special way in the soul surrendered to it, then the faculty of perception of the spiritual world is coming into existence. Then one spiritual being speaks, as it were, in one way to the soul, another in another way; and a spiritual intercourse ensues, which consists in a language of thoughts. We experience thoughts; but we know that we are experiencing beings in these thoughts. To live in beings who do not merely express themselves in thoughts, but are actually present in those thoughts with their individuality, is to live with the soul in the spiritual world.

With regard, however, to the beings of the elemental world, the soul has the feeling that they have the cosmic thoughts flowing into their own individual beings, and that they will their own existence in conformity with this universal thought streaming into them.

But with regard to the beings who need not descend to the elemental world to gain that which man can only gain in the physical world, and who attain that stage of existence in the spiritual world, the human soul has the feeling that they consist wholly of thought substance; that not only do the cosmic thoughts flow into them, but that the beings themselves actually live in that movement of thought with their individuality. They entirely allow the cosmic thoughts to think themselves within them in a living way. Their life consists in the apprehension of this cosmic language of thought, and their willing consists in their being able to express themselves in thought. This thought-existence of theirs reacts vitally upon the universe, for thoughts which are beings converse with other thoughts which are also beings.

Human thoughts are the reflection of this spiritual life of thought-beings. During the period through which the human soul passes between death and re-birth, it is woven into this life of thought-beings, just as it is woven into physical existence between birth and death. When the soul enters physical existence through birth, or rather through conception, the permanent thought-entity of the soul works in a shaping and inspiring way on the fate of that soul. In human destiny what has remained of the soul from the earth-lives preceding the present one, works in the same way as pure living thought-beings work in the universe.

When clairvoyant consciousness enters this spiritual world of living thought-beings, it feels itself to be in a completely new relationship towards the physical world. The latter confronts it in, the spiritual world as another world, just as in the physical world the spiritual world appears as another one. But to spiritual sight the physical world has lost everything which can be perceived of it within physical existence. All those qualities seem to have vanished which are grasped with the senses, or the intellect which is bound up with the senses. On the other hand, it is obvious from the standpoint of the spiritual world that the true, original nature of the physical world is itself spiritual To the soul's gaze, looking from the spiritual world, there appear instead of the previous physical world, spiritual beings unfolding their activities in such a way that through the converging of those activities that world comes into being which, looked at through the senses, is the very world that man has before him in his own physical existence. Seen from the spiritual world, the qualities, forces, materials, etc., of the physical world disappear as such, and are revealed as mere appearances. From the spiritual world man sees only beings, and in them lies true reality.

Similarly from the elemental world, when beheld from the spiritual world, there vanishes everything which is not actual being. And the soul feels that in this world too, it has to do with beings who, by letting their activities converge, cause an existence to become manifest which through the organs of sympathy and antipathy appears as elemental.

The essential part of projecting one's life into supersensible worlds consists in the fact that beings take the place of the conditions and qualities which the consciousness has around it in the physical world. The supersensible world reveals itself ultimately as a world of beings, and whatever exists in addition to those beings is the expression of their actions. Indeed, both the physical world and the elemental world appear as the deeds of spiritual beings.

XIII

The First Beginnings of Man's Physical Body

EARLIER in this book mention was made of a Moon and Sun condition, preceding the Earth condition, and only in that Moon period do there appear to clairvoyant consciousness impressions which are reminiscent of the impressions of earth-life. Such impressions are no longer to be gained when clairvoyant sight is directed to the still further distant past of the earth's Sun condition. The latter is revealed wholly as a world of beings and the actions of those beings. In order to get an impression of this Sun period, it is necessary to keep at a distance all ideas of the earth's mineral and plant life. For such ideas only have a meaning with regard to earlier conditions of the earth period; and, those of them which concern plant-life, to the long-past Moon period. To the earth's ancient Sun condition conceptions lead which may be prompted by the animal and human kingdoms of nature—conceptions, however, which do not merely portray what the senses disclose about the inhabitants of those kingdoms.

Now the clairvoyant consciousness of man finds within the etheric body active forces which form themselves into pictures of such a kind that they bring to expression the way in which the etheric body received, through the actions of spiritual beings during the ancient Sun period, its first beginning m the cosmic order of things. This beginning may be traced in its further development through the Moon and Earth periods. We find that in the course of these it was transformed, and through this transformation became what is now seen to be the active etheric body of man.

In order to understand the physical body of man, we require, however, a different activity of human consciousness. At first it appears as an outer counterpart of the etheric body. But close observation shows that man could never arrive at a complete development of his being, unless the physical body were something more than merely a physical manifestation of the etheric body. If this were so, definite willing, feeling, and thinking would take place in man, but they could not be so synthetised that the consciousness which expresses itself as an ego-experience could arise in the human soul. This becomes specially evident when the consciousness develops the quality of clairvoyance. Man's ego-experience can at first only take place in the physical world, when he is invested with his physical body. Thence he is able to take his experience into the elemental and spiritual worlds and interpenetrate his etheric and astral bodies with it. For man has an etheric and an astral body in which the ego-experience does not at first arise. Only in his physical body can that experience take place. Now if the human physical body is looked at from the spiritual world, it turns out that there is something in it, belonging to it intrinsically, which even from the spiritual world is not fully disclosed in its reality. If the consciousness enters the spiritual world in a clairvoyant capacity, the soul grows familiar with the world of thought-reality; but the ego experience, which through an adequate strengthening of soul-force may be carried into that world, is not woven simply out of universal thoughts; it does not yet feel in the world of cosmic thoughts anything in that environment which is equal to its own being. In order to feel this, the soul must advance still further into the supersensible. It must come to experiences in which it is abandoned even by thoughts, so that all physical experiences and all experiences also of thinking, feeling, and willing are, as it were, left behind it on its journey into the supersensible. Then for the first time does it feel itself one with a reality which so underlies the universe that it takes precedence of everything which man, as a physical, etheric, and

118

astral being, is able to observe. Man then feels himself in a still higher sphere than the spiritual world so far known to him. We will call this world in which only the ego can experience itself, the super-spiritual world. From it even the region of thought-reality seems an outer world. When clairvoyant consciousness is transferred to this super-spiritual world, it goes through an experience which may be described and characterised somewhat as follows, by tracing the path followed by clairvoyant consciousness through its various stages.

When the soul feels itself in its etheric body, and elemental events and beings are its environment, it knows it is outside the physical body; but that physical body still exists as an entity, although when seen from without it appears transformed. To spiritual sight a part of it becomes detached, and is manifest as the expression of the deeds of spiritual beings who have been active from the beginning of the earth's existence up to the present time. Another detached part appears as the expression of something which was already in existence during the ancient Moon condition of the earth. This state of things continues as long as the consciousness is only experiencing itself in the elemental world. In that world the consciousness is able to become aware of the way in which man was constituted as a physical being during the ancient Moon period.

When the consciousness enters the spiritual world, another part of the physical body becomes detached. It is the part which was formed during the Moon period by the deeds of spiritual beings. But another part is left behind. It is that which existed during the Sun condition of the earth as man's physical entity at that period. But even of this physical entity something is left behind, when, from the standpoint of the spiritual world, everything is taken into account which happened during the Sun period through the deeds of spiritual beings.

What is then left behind is first revealed as the action of spiritual beings when the consciousness reaches the super-spiritual world. It is revealed as already existent at the beginning of the Sun period, and we have to go back to a condition of the earth before its Sun period. In my book Occult Science, I endeavoured to vindicate the use of the term Saturn period for this condition of the earth's existence. In this sense the earth was Saturn before it became Sun. And during that Saturn period the first beginning of the physical human body came into existence out of the cosmic world-process through the deeds of spiritual beings. That beginning was afterwards so transformed during the succeeding Sun, Moon, and Earth periods by the further actions of other spiritual beings that the present physical human body became what it now is.

XIV

Concerning Man's Real Ego

WHEN the soul experiences itself in its astral body and has living thought-beings as its environment, it knows itself to be outside both the physical and etheric bodies. But it also feels that its thinking, feeling, and willing belong but to a limited sphere of the universe, whereas in virtue of its own original nature it should embrace much more than is allotted to it in that sphere. The soul that has become clairvoyant may say to itself within the spiritual world: "In the physical world I am confined to what my physical body allows me to observe; in the elemental world I am limited by my etheric body; in the spiritual world I am restricted by finding myself, as it were, upon an island in the universe and by feeling my spiritual existence bounded by the shores of that island. Beyond them is a world which I should be able to perceive if I were to work my way through the veil which is woven before the eyes of my spirit by the actions of living thought-beings." Now the soul is indeed able to work its way through this veil, if it continues to develop further and further the faculty of self surrender which is already necessary for its life in the elemental world. It is under the necessity of still further strengthening the forces which accrue to it from experience in the physical world, in order to be guarded in supersensible worlds from having its consciousness deadened, clouded, or even annihilated. In the physical world the soul, in order to experience thoughts within itself, has need only of the strength naturally allotted to it apart from its own inner work. In the elemental world thoughts, which immediately on arising fall into oblivion, are softened down to dreamlike experience, i.e. do not come into the consciousness at all, unless the soul, before entering this world, has worked on the strengthening of its inner life. For this purpose it must specially strengthen the will-power, for in the elemental world a thought is no longer merely a thought; it has an inner activity, or life of its own. It has to be held fast by the will if it is not to leave the circle of the consciousness. In the spiritual world thoughts are completely independent living beings. If they are to remain in the consciousness, the soul must be so strengthened that it develops within itself and of itself the force which the physical body develops for it in the physical world, and which in the elemental world is developed by the sympathies and antipathies of the etheric body. It must forgo all this assistance in the spiritual world. There the experiences of the physical world and the elemental world are only present to the soul as memories. And the soul itself is beyond those two worlds. Around it is the spiritual world. This world at first makes no impression upon the astral body. The soul has to learn to live by itself on its own memories. The content of its consciousness is at first merely this: "I have existed, and now I am confronting nothingness." But when the memories come from such soul-experiences as are not merely reproductions of physical or elemental occurrences, but represent free thought-experiences induced by those occurrences, there begins in the soul an exchange of thought between the memories and the supposed nothingness of the spiritual environment. And that which arises as the result of that intercourse becomes a world of conceptions in the consciousness of the astral body. The strength which is needful for the soul at this point of its development is such as will make it capable of standing on the shore of the only world hitherto known to it, and of enduring the facing of supposed nothingness. This supposed nothingness is at first an absolutely real nothingness to the soul. Yet the soul still has, so to speak, behind it the world of its memories. It can, as it were, take a firm grip of them. It can live in them. And the more it lives in them, the more it strengthens the forces of the astral body. With this strengthening begins the intercourse between its past existence and the beings of the spiritual world. During this intercourse the soul learns to feel itself as an astral being. To use an expression in keeping with ancient traditions, we may say, "The human soul experiences itself as an astral being within the cosmic Word." By the cosmic Word are here meant the thought-deeds of living thought-beings, which are enacted in the spiritual world like a living discourse of spirits; but in such a way that the discourse exactly corresponds in the spiritual world to deeds in the physical world.

If the soul now wishes to step over into the super-spiritual world, it must efface, by its own will, its memories of the physical and elemental worlds. It can only do this when it has gained the certainty, from the spirit discourse, that it will not wholly lose its existence if it effaces everything in itself which so far the consciousness of that existence has given it. The soul must actually place itself at the edge of a spiritual abyss and there make an act of will to forget its willing, feeling, and thinking. It must consciously renounce its past. The resolution that has to be taken at this point may be called a bringing about of complete sleep of the consciousness by one's own will, not by conditions of the physical or etheric body. Only this resolution must not be thought of as having for its object a return, after an interval of unconsciousness, to the same consciousness that was previously there, but as if that consciousness, by means of the resolution, really plunges into forgetfulness by its own act of will. It must be borne in mind that this process is not possible in either the physical or the elemental world, but only in the spiritual world. In the physical world the annihilation which appears as death is possible; in the elemental world there is no death. Man, in so far as he belongs to the elemental world, cannot die; he can only be transformed into another being. In the spiritual world, however, no positive transformation, in the strict sense of the word, is possible; for into whatever a human being may change, his past experience is revealed in the spiritual world as his own conscious existence. If this memory existence is to disappear within the spiritual world, it must be because the soul itself, by an act of will, has caused it to sink into oblivion. Clairvoyant consciousness is able to perform such an act of will when it has won the necessary inner strength. If it arrives at this, there emerges from the forgetfulness it has itself brought about the real nature of the ego. The super-spiritual environment gives the human soul the knowledge of that real ego. Just as clairvoyant consciousness can experience itself in the etheric and astral bodies, so too can it experience itself in the real ego.

This real ego is not created by clairvoyance; it exists in the depths of every human soul. Clairvoyant consciousness simply experiences consciously a fact appertaining to the nature of every human soul, of which it is not conscious.

After physical death man gradually lives himself into his spiritual environment. At first his being emerges into it with memories of the physical world. Then, although he has not the assistance of his physical body, he can nevertheless live consciously in those memories, because the living thought-beings corresponding to them incorporate themselves into the memories, so that the latter no longer have the merely shadowy existence peculiar to them in the physical world. And at a definite point of time between death and re-birth, the living thought-beings of the spiritual environment exert such a strong influence that, without any act of will, the oblivion which has been described is brought about. And at that moment life emerges in the real ego. Clairvoyant consciousness, by strengthening the life of the soul, brings about as a free action of the spirit that which is, so to speak, a natural occurrence between death and re-birth. Nevertheless, memory of previous earth-lives can never arise within physical experience, unless the thoughts have, during those earth-lives, been directed to the spiritual world. It is always necessary first to have known of a thing in order that a clearly recognisable remembrance of it may arise later. Therefore we must, during one earth-life, gain knowledge of ourselves as spiritual beings if we are to be justified in expecting that in our next earthly existence we shall be able to remember a former one.

Yet this knowledge need not necessarily be gained through

clairvoyance. When a person acquires a direct knowledge of the spiritual world through clairvoyance, there may arise in his soul, during the earth-lives following the one in which he gained that knowledge, a memory of the former one, in the same way in which the memory of a personal experience presents itself in physical existence. In the case, however, of one who penetrates into spiritual science with true comprehension, through without clairvoyance, the memory will occur in such a form that it may be compared with the remembrance in physical existence of an event of which he has only heard a description.

XV

Summary of Part of the Foregoing

MAN bears within him a real ego, which belongs to a super-spiritual world. In the physical world this real ego is, as it were, concealed by the experiences of thinking, feeling, and willing. Even in the spiritual world man only becomes aware of his real ego when he effaces in himself the memories of everything which he is able to experience through his thinking, feeling, and willing. The knowledge of the real ego emerges out of forgetfulness of what is experienced in the physical world, the elemental world, and the spiritual world.

The human physical body is revealed in its true nature when the soul beholds it from the super-spiritual world. Then it becomes evident that that body first took its rise out of the universal cosmic process during a Saturn period which preceded the Sun period of the earth. Subsequently, during the Sun, Moon, and Earth periods, it developed into what the human physical body is at present.

In accordance with the foregoing, man's collective being may be expressed in tabular form as follows:

I. The physical body in the environment of the physical world. By its means man recognises himself as an independent individual being or ego. This physical body was formed, at its first beginning, from the universal cosmic essence during a long-past Saturn period of the earth, and through its development during four planetary metamorphoses of the earth has become what it now is.

II. The subtle, etheric body in the elemental environment. By its means man recognises himself as a member of the earth's elemental or vital body. This body was formed, at its first beginning, from the universal cosmic essence during a long-past Sun period of the earth, and through its development during three planetary metamorphoses of the earth has become what it now is.

III. The astral body in a spiritual environment. Through it man is a member of a spiritual world. In it is situated man's other self which realises itself in repeated earth-lives.

IV. The real ego in a super-spiritual environment. In this man finds himself as a spiritual being, even when all experiences of the physical, elemental, and spiritual worlds, and therefore all experiences of the senses and of thinking, feeling, and willing, sink into oblivion.

XVI

Remarks on the Connection of what is described in this Book with the Accounts given in my Books Theosophy and Occult Science

NAMES which are to express the experiences of the human soul in the elemental and spiritual worlds must be adapted to the special characteristics of those experiences. In giving such names it will have to be borne in mind that even in the elemental world experience runs its course in quite a different way from that in which it does in the physical world. Experience in the elemental world is due to the soul's capacity for transformation and to its observation of sympathies and antipathies. The terminology will necessarily assume something of the changeful character of such experiences. It cannot be as fixed and rigid as it must be with regard to the physical world. One who does not keep in view this fact, arising out of the nature of the case, may easily find a contradiction between the terminology used in this book and that in Theosophy and Occult Science. The contradiction disappears when it is remembered that in the two latter works the names are so chosen that they characterise those experiences which the soul has during its complete development between birth (conception) and death on the one hand, and between death and re-birth on the other. In this book, however, the names are given with reference to the experiences of clairvoyant consciousness when it enters the elemental world and the spiritual spheres.

It is seen from Theosophy and Occult Science that soon after the detachment of the physical body from the soul at death, there is also detached from the soul that which in this book is called the etheric body. The soul then lives for a while in the entity which is here called the astral body. The etheric body, after being detached from the soul, is transformed within the elemental world. It passes into the beings forming that world. When this transformation of the etheric body takes place, the soul which had lived in it is no longer there. The soul, however, experiences as its outer world after death the processes of the elemental world. This experience of the elemental world "from without" is described in Theosophy and Occult Science as the passage of the soul through the "soul-world." It must therefore be realised that this soul-world is identical with that which, from the standpoint of clairvoyant consciousness, is in this book called the elemental world.

When the soul in the interval between death and re-birth—as described in Theosophy—becomes detached from its astral body, it goes on living in the entity which is here called the real ego. The astral body then experiences by itself, the soul being no longer with it, that which has been described above as oblivion. It plunges, so to speak, into a world in which there is nothing which can be observed with the senses, or experienced in the way in which will, feeling and thought, as man develops them in his physical body, experience things. This world is experienced as its outer world by the soul which continues to exist in the real ego. If it is desirable to characterise the experience in this outer world, it can be done in the same way in which it is described in Theosophy and Occult Science, as the passing through the "spirit region." The soul, experiencing itself in the real ego, has around it within the spiritual world that which has been formed in it as soul-experiences during physical existence. Within the world above described as that of living thoughts-beings, the soul finds between death and re-birth all that it has experienced in its inner being during physical existence through its sense perceptions and its thinking, feeling, and willing.

Printed in Great Britain
by Amazon

43921952R00081